Myths of Time and History

A Unitarian Universalist Theology

by
Alice Blair Wesley

Copyright 1987 by Alice Blair Wesley

First Printing, September 1987
Second Printing, August 1988

All rights reserved. No part of this book may be reproduced by any means without the prior written permission of the author. All author's rights under the copyright laws will be strictly enforced.

Design and Typography by:
Words Unlimited, Inc.
4 Old Stable Lane, Newark, DE 19711
(302) 368-4177

Printed in the United States of America.

Contents

Introduction
1

The Story of My Wrestling with Stories
9

In and Out of the Transcendent Realm of the Imagination and Back in the Mundane with a Difference
31

An Old Story Re-told: Lessons Learned in the Wilderness After Liberation
51

A Theology of Time and Character: Classical Unitarian Christian Theology of History
69

The Pilgrims and the Spirit of the Covenant of the Free Church
89

Conclusion
113

Introduction

Meanings of words change.

In the history of language and ideas, a very significant widening of worldview may sometimes be brought to focus in the shifted meaning of a single word. In our century, myth is such a word.

In our century liberal scholars — of the Bible, other art and literature, theology, church history, anthropology, sociology and world religions — have increasingly used the word myth to mean, most simply: any culture-shaping story. The definition must be amplified. Stated so briefly it doesn't say much. What makes a story culture-shaping?

The initial point to be made, however, is this: As 20th century scholars use it, the word myth does not any longer mean a story betraying misconceptions naively inherited from the fanciful past.

Those who still use the word myth with that meaning show themselves unaware of the widened worldview of which the shifted meaning is a part. With their usage they disclose the particular story of time and history they hold, the myth of progress. In the 19th century the myth of progress — a story in which Europeans and North Americans were "leading" characters — shaped much of European and American culture.

It was then that we began to use the word myth to derogate *others'* stories. Those who still use the word myth with that meaning almost surely picture their own religion — or lack of religion — as located at a narrow apex of cultural development, not within the wider universe of religion and culture. That meaning is a function of *one* culture-shaping myth among many. The word is of much older vintage.

As 20th century scholars use it, the word myth has no polemical overtones, any more than does the word formula, say, for a physicist. You would not hear a physicist say, as though idiocy and belief in formulas were synonymous, "That idiot believes in a formula!" No more does a humanities scholar — who lives intellectually in the 20th century — say disparagingly of any, "They hold myths to be true!"

On the contrary, scholars who write, for example, of the myth of the Christ, or of the Buddha, or of the covenant may themselves devoutly believe in the validity of the myth under discussion. They may at the same time be very critical of aspects of the myth or of interpretations of the myth, as readily as any physicist might criticize some variable in a formula as in need of correction. But no physicist suggests there could be such a thing as physics without formulas. No more does the humanities scholar now imply, with the use of the word myth, there could ever be human culture without myths.

This book on myths of time and history is written for North American Unitarian Universalists, but the myths belonging to us belong to our whole culture generally. And what *liberals* now do with the myths of our common culture — how we interpret and tell and transmit them — is more like than different, whether we are liberal Jews, Catholics, Protestants or (as the check-only-one forms say) Other.

This is so as a result of a sweeping reformation in Western scholarship. It has crossed all boundaries of particular religious groups. It has altered the identifying mark of liberal thought. No religious groups ever have been monolithic. All, including ours, have always included members ranging from reactionary to liberal. Width and rigor of view has long distinguished the one from the other. What more precisely distinguishes theological liberals from theological reactionaries now, is a grasp of the concept known as historical consciousness.

Comparable in the humanities to $E=mc^2$ in the physical sciences, the term historical consciousness signifies a watershed shift in perspective and a very significantly expanded worldview. It amounts to a changed understanding of all religion and culture, faith and language, and the mutual relationship between our myths and the structures — metaphysical and social — within which we human beings think and live. For decades liberal scholars in many communions have been making prodigious efforts to teach their members to see themselves and their heritage from this perspective and within a widened worldview. And they have made much headway.

Liberals treasure and see as vitally necessary — they don't resent or bemoan — particularity. Our myths belong to us in particular ways and to others in other particular ways. But these are so inherently and dynamically related, from the perspective of historical consciousness, as to be inseparable from the larger culture, or tradition, within which all particular groups participate in continuously mutual interaction. The reason for the scholars' prodigious efforts is this: Once historical consciousness is achieved, we see that self-understanding cannot be properly said to exist — we don't know who we are or what we ought to be doing — apart from an understanding of many mutually influencing factors, within and among particular groups, of the larger whole. Nor can we understand people of the past apart from the many mutually influencing factors of their times.

It is that — the importance of many mutually influencing

factors — the illiberal cannot see. And so they react against a wider view. They see it as a dangerous threat to the identity they have more narrowly defined, "independently" not interdependently.

"How dare you assert our conceptions are related to the varying (specifically historical) dynamics of culture and tradition? We deal with universally timeless (unvarying, unhistorical) truth. Our tradition is not a part of any other!" So the illiberal everywhere, in effect, cry, resisting the relativity of historical consciousness.

This book aims to speak to three questions, though far from exhaustively. (1) Why is it Unitarian Universalists have been slower than others to achieve a historical consciousness? (2) What are the principal myths of the larger tradition of which ours is a part? And (3) in what particular ways do these myths belong to Unitarian Universalists? Or, how does a liberal Unitarian Universalist interpret, tell and transmit them?

I have deliberately not written in the conventional scholarly mode. The chapters are without detailed references and there are few footnotes. There are thousands of works of scholarship on the issues I discuss. If you want, you may easily find them. But most of us don't read works of scholarship outside our own fields. Outside our own fields they usually strike us as dense, opaque. I have wanted to write instead readable — even enjoyable — essays for our members, for lay theologians.

I tell, or rather re-tell, several stories from the perspective which I also talk about. So this is partly a storybook, as well as a book *about* myths. It is so because that's what I think it *must be* if the book is to fulfill its purpose, which is: to help more Unitarian Universalists achieve both a historical consciousness and historical consciousness *of* our myths. I don't think these can be communicated separately. Here's why.

Myths are somewhat like the formulas of physics. Coming

to understand myths from the perspective of a historical consciousness is somewhat like making the shift from Newtonian to Einsteinian physics. Myths formulate the worldviews which make common cultures possible. Yet unlike formulas, myths are stories, a form of art. People just don't "take in" formulas and art in the same way.

Somebody once asked the great jazz trumpeter Louis Armstrong, "What is jazz?" Louie's face lit up with his famously wide smile and he replied, "Man, if you have to ask, you ain't ever gonna know!"

Louie was a great artist, not a musicologist. His reply is not quite entirely accurate. Conceivably, a learned musicologist could learn what jazz is by questioning the systematic work of another musicologist, without ever hearing any. But Louie was right practically. If jazz is a different kind of music from what you have previously understood music to be, the way to learn what jazz is, is to listen to jazz. Similarly, the way to learn what myths are, from a different perspective than you have yet grasped, is to listen to stories told — so to speak — "in that genre of the art." Premature questions will lack the "syncopation" of the subject; so their answers will not make sense to you. You'd better first listen to the stories. If you insist on asking questions first, "you ain't ever gonna know."

But then myths are only somewhat like jazz. We don't learn the meaning of myths *just* by listening to narratives, as to jazz, any more than students of physics learn relativity physics just by listening to a physicist recite formulas. Myths and formulas require interpretation. Each is part and parcel of the other, without which the other is meaningless.

All that about myths, formulas and jazz to try here to indicate why this book is not systematic in the sense some might wish, who wanted to begin by asking, "What is myth?" I intend to be the more effective, of course, for mixing explanation and story as I have. I hope that is the case.

Pondering what to say in this Introduction, I remembered a conversation with Prof. Ron Bryan, a physicist on the faculty of Texas A&M University in College Station, Texas, home also of my first parish.

Ron said something like this: Relativity physics is simple. It's really very, very simple. The shift from Newtonian to Einsteinian physics is small, but subtle. And some of the students have a terrible time with it at first, for just that reason. They can either look at everything a little differently, or they can't. They either get it, or they don't. If they do, I can cover scads of material in the first course. If they don't, I have to slow way down and take it all step by step. Then one day there's this little click. They see! Then they can catch up with the others very quickly. But sometimes I have to make a whole course of something I could otherwise explain in about fifteen minutes.

Ron initiated this conversation after an evening class I was teaching in 20th century liberal theology. He was one of the students. But in any partnership of equals, an exchange of roles can happen at any time, in the blink of an eye. That had happened. Ron had become the teacher and I the student. He was trying to teach the minister how to teach theology.

He went on to say: I get glimmers of this different perspective you're trying to show us from which everything about religion looks different to you, makes more sense to you than it does to me, and is really simple — like relativity physics is to me. But you need to slow way down and take it step by step. I'm not getting it yet.

That conversation was in 1977. You might say this book is the fruit of it, and dozens of others with other seriously inquiring members of our churches and fellowships.

I have taken Ron's instruction seriously. I think I will never be able to "take it step by step" in just the way he may have meant I should. My method is rather to start over, repeatedly, each time playing a variation on the combination of explanation and story, perhaps rather more like Satchmo after all than like Ron in his lecture hall.

But then, it happens Ron and his wife Mary, when I knew them, were not only professors of physics and logic respectively, but also exquisite jazz musicians, he a pianist and she a drummer. So I hope yet to teach members like them well, or at least better, for having had his and many other members' helpful tutoring.

Parts of the first chapter are from a paper read before the Harper's Ferry Study Group of Unitarian Universalist Ministers and published in the *Unitarian Universalist Christian*, there titled "On Language of the Holy." The four chapters following began as sermons, delivered in various permutations. Then all five chapters were a series of five lectures delivered to Unitarian Universalists attending the Connecticut Valley District's Week at Ferry Beach in the summer of 1986. Those hearing the lectures were warmly enthusiastic in their response. I have made few changes in adapting them for readers. I rather hope their originally oral character lingers.

I am grateful to the Adele Abrahamse, Carole Etzler and the Rev. John Corrado for permission to quote their lyrics.

I thank good friends and colleagues, the Rev. Prof. James Luther Adams, and the Rev. Drs. Forrester Church, Gordon McKeeman and David Rankin, who read the manuscript and graciously offered comments, some of which I heeded and some I did not. Blame the book's deficiencies on my decisions.

1

The Story of My Wrestling with Stories

———•••●●●•••———

This is a book about myths. I shall be trying to show you a way of seeing the whole subject of religious experience, culture, institutions and history — as all these flow from and through our myths — which I expect will seem revolutionary to some.

"Revolutionary" has a drastic sound. I do not intend to be drastic. On the contrary, I'd like you to think, for example, of a small shift in the angle of a your holding a kaleidoscope. You know the elements inside a kaleidoscope remain the same. The little bits of colored rock inside, and the mirrors, do not change. But if you turn a kaleidoscope just a little bit — a few degrees — you will see an entirely changed pattern.

In trying to explain a contemporary, scholarly view of myths to Unitarian Universalists, I have sometimes felt tremendous resistance, as though my listeners think I am out to displace the world of thought they are familiar with and replace it with a foreign one. Actually, I am simply trying to get them to look at the stories of religion from a different angle, with a small difference that does indeed make a great difference, but not nearly so great as some might fear.

Myths of Time and History: A Unitarian Universalist Theology. That's my title. I might have called this series of essays "A Rational Defense and Critique of the Religious Imagination: Or, How We Human Beings Use Wonderfully Imaginative Stories to Inform Ourselves About and Deal With Reality."

The key words are: rational, imaginative and reality. Myths are imaginative stories. Human beings use myths as vehicles or tools for understanding and negotiating reality. We may understand our use of myths in a rational, not at all debunking, way.

Note please: The word imaginative does not necessarily mean: fanciful or fantastic. Some myths are fanciful and fantastic. Others are derived from or incorporate elements of actual history. Yet, it takes just as much imagination to remember, understand and tell a historical, plainly factual story as a fanciful or fantastic story. Either type of story — fanciful or historical, or a story *combining* fanciful and historical elements — may or may not be properly called mythical. A mythical story is one people of a given social group consciously or implicitly acknowledge to be freighted with the very meaning of life. It's the *freight* a story carries that makes it religious, hence a people's myth.

For people who consciously, or only implicitly, hold a particular story or myth to be valid, the story has a bearing on everything, on the ways of all things creative and/or destructive in present experience, even on those things assigned to a category neither creative nor destructive, but merely trivial, of little concern.

The following is a definition I'll be using throughout. A *vitalizing* myth is a story about the vitalizing forces of existence and about those other forces tending toward destruction, with which the vitalizing forces more successfully than unsuccessfully contend.

There are also myths, versions of myths and interpretations of myths which may be criticized as *not* vitalizing, but restrictive, constrictive, even killing. That, of course, is the reason for trying to get some handles on the subject. Myths matter, greatly.

For example, in no good, vitalizing myths are the "good guys" able simply to conquer the "ogres" absolutely. If they do, those who hold the myth to be valid will sooner or later prove blind to the complexity of whatever the myth points to as "bad." And that is bad for everybody. That is what happened, for instance, with the myth of progress held valid by technologically "superior" Westerners. Believing that myth, some technologically "superior" Westerners *still* can't see the full, complex humanity of "Third World" peoples. But more of the myth of progress later.

You may take these first few pages as an introduction to this first chapter. I hoped some introductory remarks might be helpful, but I don't like starting out so abstractly. It makes sense to me to believe the reason we human beings are such inveterate myth makers and story tellers, is that we can communicate reality *far* more richly and dramatically with stories, and more *easily*, than we do when we talk prosaic abstraction. So now I'd like to start over, with a story — mine.

I will begin by telling you the story of my personal religious journey. My reasons are two. First, you'll see more of where I'm coming from right from the start if I tell you my story. Secondly, my personal religious story is, very much, a story of wrestling with the stories — or myths — of our religious culture. Better than if I had begun with a string of ever so precise definitions, you will pick up the meaning of terms I use from the context of my unfolding story.

• • •

To tell you the personal story of Alice Blair Wesley, I must begin in the 17th century.[1]

In the 17th century some English speaking commoners got

hold of the Bible in their own language. They surely already knew some of the stories. But it was only when they read the stories for themselves and discussed them among themselves that they learned from them what they did of their own *personal* nature. Please understand: From my experience of their heirs, the main thing these common folk of the 17th century took from the Bible was an extraordinarily heightened sense of the worth and dignity of the common individual.

I'll put that in terms they themselves used. They learned from the Bible that anyone who could read or understand the proclaimed Word of the Gospel, could surrender in freedom to the Holy Spirit, the powerful, loving spirit of God Almighty, Creator of the world, active *in them* as individuals. And as individuals, every detail of whose personhood was the loving concern of the Father— As individuals, they could know and then share the fellowship of others who know, the influx of a transforming glory so rich as to be beyond description except in song, yet a glory only dimly prophetic, a foretaste of the glory certain someday to be theirs as adopted children of the King, heirs, brothers and sisters of Christ the elder brother, risen and exalted eternally.

The significance of these 17th century Anabaptists for all later Western history was very great, indeed. For they, and other left-wing religious radicals, invented a form of church government called congregational polity. In Chapter 5 I'll be talking about another group of these radicals, the Pilgrims of Scrooby, Leyden and Plymouth, spiritual ancestors of American Unitarians. The basic political idea of these radicals was that individuals in the local church, commoners or not, worthy of the indwelling presence of the Holy Spirit of God Almighty, were certainly worthy enough to run their own affairs in the church. They, therefore, didn't need any higher-ups — bishops — to order them around. But more of that later, too.

The significance of these 17th century Anabaptists *for me*

was that some of them migrated to Virginia and later moved through the Cumberland Gap into the hills and valleys of Southeastern Kentucky, thereby dropping into something like a deep pocket of the greatcoat of the Western world. These were my people.

The King James Bible was published early in the 17th century, in 1611. The Anabaptist interpretation of the Bible produced a religious and political revolution, part of the Reformation. My family's migration to Kentucky was part of the Reformation. But life in Kentucky farm country was little changed by anything that happened after that. At the beginning of the 19th century, their hero Thomas Jefferson was elected President. (I can barely resist inserting here something about the fascinating confluence of Baptist and Enlightenment piety in Jefferson's election, but I must.) In the 19th century there was the great War Between the States. But these and other large events of the history books, preserved rather than changed the status quo of their community, their "world."

From 1611 to 1940 the only epoch-shaping thing that happened in Southeastern Kentucky was that the inheritors of the revolution forgot the revolution. They had no notion of the Reformation. They couldn't have told you when it happened or where or who any of the leaders were or what were any of the philosophical or political issues involved in that upheaval. The only trace of the Reformation in memory was a hatred of Catholicism.

Here's another way of saying what happened. The people forgot the world shaping implications of their own ancestors' interpretation of their sacred stories, their myths. They became what Mircea Eliade called, in his book *The Myth of the Eternal Return*[2], an archaic society. That is: They were conscious of a certain amount of "history." They read the newspapers and listened to news reports on the radio; they knew something of what was happening in the outside world. Yet religiously, they made every effort to disregard history. Theirs was a privatized revolt *against* concrete, historical time. They lived rather by the spiritual resources of continual return to the "Great Time," the time of the beginning of the ministry of Christ. That ministry was, in their understanding, the same, unchanging, an inexhaustible source of refreshment and encouragement, in their own time.

The people were, as it were, historically enchanted. Round about 1650 an Irish archbishop, James Ussher, published a biblical genealogy. By listing all the generations mentioned in the Hebrew Scriptures and estimating their ages, Ussher concluded — around 1650 — that the world was created in 4004 B.C.E. My father never heard Ussher's name, nor did he know of any other biblical scholarship. But he had got the idea, from he knew not where, that the events of the first chapter of Genesis took place around 4000. Two thousand years later came Moses, he believed, and two thousand years after Moses came Jesus. It has now been almost 2000 years since Jesus' First Coming.

Now according to the Gospels, Jesus explicitly forbade speculation on the dating of the Last Days which only the Father, not even the Son, knows. But the appeal of symmetry is strong. In sheepish defiance of Christ's prohibition on making much of such figures, my father, a country Baptist preacher, expected the Second Coming around the year 2000. Such then was his schedule, his periodization, of the beginning, middle and end of the story — or myth — of the world.

In the 1940's the year 2000 was just near enough at hand to be exciting, though not immediately anticipated. The violence and glory of the end-time of judgment lent a kind of glowing urgency to the Gospel without scary threat, just as songs about heaven heightened the value of to-be-exalted individuals while suppressing pridefulness, the prideful being forbidden entrance.

The mind of the Southeastern American fundamentalist is unaware that anything has happened within its 6000 year timeframe of history fundamentally to challenge its understanding of things human and/or divine. The people do not know the specific history of their ideas, such as that the 6000 year timeframe itself was only formulated in the 17th century, that it is not *a given* among students of the Bible, but an arguable issue. Life for that mind has not changed since the departure from Eden. Life is taken to be now about as it was for the ancient Israelites or for St. Paul and the early church. Those who do not see the redeeming and sanctifying truths of the holy are simply those heedlessly given over to worldly pursuits. In the 1940s even Hitler, Tojo and the Communists, far off, seemed more or less like the far off evil rulers of biblical times.

In their own years, to be sure, there were technical changes. (And it is fascinating to note that with a part of their minds, they accepted the specifically American — not Christian — civil myth, according to which these technical changes somehow proved the "superiority" of the United States. Southern American fundamentalists are intensely patriotic even while regarding the majority of their fellow citizens as fully meriting everlasting damnation. This makes sense when you understand the relationship between their peculiar and particular version of the Christian myth and the American civil myth.) In their own years, mines were tunneled, telephone wires strung, automobiles and picture shows brought in, and fine new roads cut and paved.

Yet even in the early 1940s — only four decades ago — my grandfathers and uncles walked behind horses to plow; my grandmothers and aunts drew water from wells hand over hand with rope and pulley. Everybody washed hands and faces on the back porch. On Saturdays they bathed in Number 2 washtubs before wood burning cookstoves in the kitchen.

There were murders and accidents, flu epidemics and

cancers. There was the never-ending and all-encompassing gossip of intense, small-community life. (They were as gossipy as our small Unitarian Universalist community.) There were urgent contests for the county judgeship, occasional windfalls of high prices for bumper crops as well as fearful drops in tobacco and corn and coal prices. There were, reliably, the great pleasures of Southern cooking for keenly hungry, hard-working people, the many thrills — vicarious and immediate — of love affairs, and the unfailing delights of babies and young children.

Yet, as in all times, as they thought, since the 1st century of the new dispensation in Christ, when they reached an age of accountability, conviction and conversion, they were baptized by immersion for the remission of their sins in the area's rivers. And regularly on Sundays there was the ecstasy of preaching and testimony and hymn. And how they did sing! The Lord's day was holy unto the Lord and to the people.

A student of religion asks: "What was the nature of that ecstasy in the heart of this particular cult, or sub-cult, of our culture in which the myths — or stories — of ancient Israel, Christ and the early church, were told over and over again?"

Great scholars of religion of our time, such as Eliade or Rudolph Otto or Clifford Geertz[3], have maintained that a group's experience of the holy can only be known either from inside the group, or by students having at their disposal *both* a highly informed grasp of the whole social context of the experience *and* a keenly sympathetic imagination. Please note two principal assumptions of contemporary scholarship: (1) Another people's religious experience is *difficult* to understand because it is is enmeshed in their whole social context, and human social contexts vary tremendously. Therefore, we ought to hold suspect any too *facile* interpretations. Yet, (2) understanding of another people's religious experience *is* theoretically possible because universally common human nature is a reality. There is no evidence that human nature has changed in historical times. Therefore, we can, with enough information, imagine and apprehend the religions of both ancient peoples and contemporary cultures outside our own.

Shortly, I shall try to tell you what the ecstatic experience, at the heart of this sub-cult of Christianity, was like for me as the insider I was at a thirteen years of age in 1949.

But for a moment consider conclusions that might have been drawn by an intelligent outsider looking on at the Sunday observance of these, my people, and looking for *operational* meanings of the word holy in the 1940s when I was a child. An outsider might have assessed the word holy operationally to mean any of the following.

Holy meant clean; for on Sundays the people were scrubbed and shining. Holy meant sorrowful; for consciousness of sin — of selfishness or temper or sensuality — brought agonizing bouts of conscience and painful regret. Holy meant jubilant and affectionate; for on Sundays there was hand clapping and foot patting and embracing and much singing. Holy meant sexually arousing; for on Sundays flirtation and courting went on everywhere, discreetly and not so discreetly. Holy meant self-assuring; for the people of this God-saturate community were — and still are — amazingly confident of their opinions, downright scornful of all external authorities. And holy meant restful; for on Sunday afternoons it was right to yield to bone-weary fatigue and leave the fields and kitchens and shops untended. Mercifully, in late afternoons on the Lord's Day idleness was not sloth, and the righteous could rest. By that vitalizing power made available through the telling of their myths — stories — all these aspects of their lives were made holy, affirmed, sanctified, cherished, unreservedly revered.

Yet these aspects of the holy, visible to an astute outside observer, did not constitute the most intensely personal experience at the core of the cult. That I learned on a Sunday morning near the end of a service in the city when I was thirteen. In the terms used inside the mythical structures under discussion, that experience came with my acceptance of Jesus as my personal savior. Of course, I did not learn until years later that any scholars had tried to put this experience in terms that would cover theoretically the experience of the holy in many human societies. So, I'm getting way ahead of my story in using such terms at this point.

Nevertheless, I will say here what happened when I was thirteen, using now Eliade's terms. Having heard the language of the symbols, myths and rites of my religious culture all my life up to that point with — as it were — an outer ear, I suddenly understood them as "a complex system of coherent affirmations about the ultimate reality of things," a metaphysics, *in which I was a participant* and, therefore, ultimately real myself. That was the good news, the Gospel. I was expected, upon understanding the Gospel, profoundly to regret or repent that I had ever behaved or acted as though I didn't belong — which I heartily did. Then I *really* belonged. I knew myself to be a worthy individual, fully accepted by and through divine action. I became in a sense "new." I was newly "real" through participation in the prototypes of the "original ontology" revealed in the stories about the "primordial acts of the gods" — in this case God the Father, Christ the Son and the Holy Spirit — at the "beginning" of the church. (All these phrases set off by quotation marks Eliade used to describe archaic religion in many cultures.)

According to another story — or myth — of history, quite outside the ken of those among whom I was born, according to Karl Marx's myth, the material, technical changes introduced into my world should have made a great difference in the worldview possible to one growing up in that world. And indeed they did, eventually.

In 1940 my father and mother had lost their farm. The effects of the Great Depression were yet very potent. My father had been out of work for two years. In 1940, when I was four years old, increased production related to the War in Europe meant that Dad could get on at the railroad shops in Louisville. Along with many millions of others, we were propelled out of reach of the land by the economics of the Depression and World War II. In 1940 we moved to the city, and there began my slow wrench from the 17th century into the 20th.

I stayed in the church of my family for the first twenty-three years of my life. I don't think I need to describe how I came to leave, mostly because many a Unitarian Universalist has traveled such a path. If you don't know what it's like, ask around in nearly any UU discussion group. My path involved disgust for and an angry rejection of what I slowly learned in the city to see as their anti-intellectualism, their nationalism, their massive provincialism, their racism, and their personally inhibiting, literally maddening sexism.

Instead of describing the negative consequences of the religious sub-culture into which I was born, as I learned to see them, I want to try to describe something else I believe is much more important for contemporary religious liberals, in significant numbers, to come to understand. And that is a way seeing the role of myths in our lives *both* critically *and* positively.

The nasty *-isms* I listed, anti-intellectualism, provincialism, sexism and so on: These were certainly in part spiritual products of the immersion of my family in their particular religious myths. Yet, I hope you heard in my account of their "world" much else, very positive, besides: an extraordinary hallowing of the worth of the individual, some ideas that are the *root* ideas of political democracy in our culture, and a profoundly enriching reverence for certain aspects of *any* healthy personal or communal life.

My thesis is: With a better understanding of the relation

between these positive features and their myth, we liberals could do a *much better* job of building on the positive features *and* combatting the *-isms*.

Further, I will insert here the principal thesis of this entire presentation: Myths are central in all human life. All people and all cultures without exception hold myths to be true. Any who believe that others — less sophisticated — may naively hold myths to be true while they themselves do not, are themselves naive.[4]

The question is not: Do we hold myths to be true, but *which* do we hold and why?[5] What is the specific history of our myths and the links between them? What are the implications of the myths we and others hold? How can we get conscious of these? And how can we be both critical and respectful of our own and others' myths, *so that* we can work within the mythical structures of the cult for positive change in the culture?

I continue with the story of how I came to see these questions as so important. I skip to the year 1962. I was a Unitarian by this time, having joined our Louisville Church in 1960. By 1962 my husband Joe and I had moved to Delaware, and I had begun graduate studies in literature.

I was heavy into Greek drama of the 5th and 4th centuries B.C.E. You might say I had a passionate love affair going, with ancient Athens. As a student of literature I was reading the dramas produced at the great festivals of the god Dionysos. I read all the extant plays of Aeschylus, Sophocles, Euripides, and Aristophanes, some forty-seven counting a few which only survive as fragments. I read them carefully and repeatedly. I looked up in handbooks every allusion to legendary and mythical characters and events. I read around the 5th century, backwards and forward, the pre- and post-Socratic philosophers and historians and some of the Roman writers. I read all the secondary critical literature in English I could lay hands on. I was at an impasse. The plays did not make sense. Neither did the interpreters, critics like Gilbert Murray and Jane Harrison.

Then one day I read in translation Nietzsche's *Birth of Tragedy*, the first half of it anyway.[6] I experienced a sudden astounding insight. I reeled. I hardly slept for weeks. I was exploding with talk I couldn't make anybody I knew understand, not even my very patient major professor at the University of Delaware, Dr. Cyrus Day. I had stumbled into reading religious literature *as literature*, art.

The deities of ancient Greek religion were *real*! They were the live imaginative personifications by which the people of a vibrantly alive culture had talked about, understood and embodied the creative and destructive forces operative in the dynamic life of their souls and society. And Plato! Plato and his Sophist opponents — the prosaic philosophers — had killed these deities. Speakers and writers of abstract prose killed the imaginative, poetic fiction of religious art: the gods and goddesses, nymphs and titans, heroes and heroines of Greek life. And Greek culture, the most rational, effulgent, creative effervescent achievement of the ancient Western world, died with them, a long lingering death.

The critics I had been reading did not understand what had happened, it seemed and still seems, to me. Because these 20th century interpreters viewed the abstract prose of Socrates and Plato as some kind of "advance" on popular religion, their assessment of ancient Greek culture was horribly skewed. Their interpretations of the myths and the plays were a kind of parody of Greek religion.

This encounter with ancient Greek religious art immediately transformed for me the legendary and mythical characters and events of my own culture. Whatever may be their mix of historical fact and fancy, I saw that the legendary and mythical characters and events of our stories must be understood as figures of *true* fiction, *art*. Adam and Eve, Yahweh and Abraham, Moses, Miriam, Pharoah and the Wilderness, Isaiah and the Christ, Mary and all the saints ... George Washington and the cherry tree, Paul Bunyan and John Henry and Santa Claus took on fresh, existentially powerful meaning.

These figures, these characters in our vitalizing myths, are re-presentations of reality. Reality presents itself to our senses. But we don't "get it" in big enough chunks to integrate very much of it or make sense of it. So through art we re-present the real, present it in a different mode, in stories — myths. The hyphenated term, re-present, is Paul Ricoeur's. He uses it to make the crucial point: Our myths do not *merely* represent reality. Rather they re-present reality itself in a mode we can apprehend. Through them we meet — face to face as it were — and learn to deal with the vitalizing forces of existence and of those other forces tending toward destruction.

We could have no culture, no civilization without these stories. For a culture *is*: a group of people who remember and argue over and continuously, creatively re-interpret imaginative stories — myths.[7]

I began to see the degree to which the "Platos and Sophists" of our era have succeeded in a work very like that of a time when another great civilization ended. In our era, as in Hellenistic times, few of the educated leaders of society take the ancient inherited myths seriously. The educated do not see that they have not discarded myths, but have only taken up others, some of these not vitalizing. Many of the educated have cut themselves off from the disciplines of the tradition, from dialogue with the best minds of the Western world of other centuries as these struggled with healthy ways of interpreting and applying the lessons of our myths. The educated have, of course, simultaneously cut themselves off from dialogue with the masses of people, who still *do* take our ancient myths seriously, and abandoned them to religious leaders who are irrational at best, if not outright charlatans and demagogues. Hence, ours is a century of spiritual cleavage and crisis.

All this came upon me in a rush in the autumn and winter of the 1962-63 academic term. I am still struggling to express it coherently. But though I arrived at this view of the mythical confusion in our culture by myself, I am by no means alone in it. However, I did not know *that* until early in 1974, when I began to study for the Unitarian Universalist ministry with the Rev. Prof. James Luther Adams at Meadville/Lombard Theological School in Chicago. I began to learn then how widely this view is shared by liberal theologians — Jewish, Roman Catholic, Protestant and even secular — and has been widely shared for some 60 to 100 years.

Our 20th century religious situation is one of fierce competition among different myths, having different presuppositions, different characters, and different periodizations of history. Our times have seen many efforts to come up with new and common vocabularies for discussing our common problems and aspirations. I see our recent Unitarian Universalist effort to reformulate our Principles and Purposes in this context, as one more effort of some of the "best and brightest" to find language for authentic discussion of what is ultimately real and important.

Yet, well-intentioned and "right on" as I believe our efforts are — that's why I'm still Unitarian Universalist — our efforts fail to communicate with people of the culture at large. I believe this is so because — and will remain so as long as — the characters of our myth are but abstractions, without explicit story.

The characters of our implicit UU myth are: the inherent worth and dignity of every individual, the covenant of congregational polity, and the interdependent web of existence of which we are a part. These terms are but our transpositions of traditional theology, discussed for centuries under the rubrics of the nature of humanity, the nature of the Church and the nature of God. Our terms have been abstracted *from* concrete, imaginative stories, myths, e.g., from the stories of of the Exodus and the Prophets, of the Prodigal Son and the Lost Sheep, of the Pilgrims and the Puritans, and of Yahweh, Lord of (interdependent) Creation and History, who must not be imaged lest the representation of the Divine itself become an idol. However, most Unitarian Universalists don't understand our links with these stories, or know from where our abstract "characters" came.

Ironically, in some ways Unitarian Universalists — perhaps the most degreed of any religious group on the North American continent — have become as historically provincial as my father. He didn't know he got his 6000 year time-frame from James Ussher. Few Unitarian Universalists know the historical sources of our myths.

We need to reclaim our myths — in their concreteness — not only so that we can better communicate as liberals with others in our culture who interpret these same myths narrowly and even meanly, but also so that we can, with a better appreciation of our own myths, be more profoundly sensitive to those of other cultures.

In the remainder of this first chapter, I want to deal with concepts I learned from two scholars, Paul Ricoeur and Jim Adams, namely: the character of a myth as an extended metaphor and, hence, the strengths and the built-in defects of any myth. These two concepts I have found helpful in my own efforts to be both critical and positive in dealing with our own and others' myths.[8]

First, Ricoeur says we must understand all the intricacies of event and plot in a myth — or imaginative story — as an extended metaphor. What is a metaphor? It is a poetic figure by which a thing of large embrace — e.g., God or the whole universe — or a large class of things is spoken of as being *like* a familiar, smaller thing. Wide acceptance of a genuinely new metaphor is a major event in the life of a culture because a new metaphor opens up vast new vistas to novel exploration, though it may also shut down others.

Take for example the impact of Newton's metaphor: The universe is like a machine which everywhere and at all times operates according to regular laws which may be observed, tested and measured. Widespread acceptance of that metaphor — which we call the scientific revolution — has sent Westerners looking religiously in all directions for measurable laws, and wonderfully, how many have been found! That is the strength of the mechanical metaphor.

However, this metaphor also precipitated a myth of the universe, not like a machine in some very important ways, but *as* a machine in all ways. The defect of this metaphor is that it leaves out those parts of reality *unlike* a machine, e.g., the human experience of compassion. But a myth uncritically accepted as totally encompassing *all* reality can actually cause us not to *see* or credit as ontologically — or *really* — significant, crucially significant elements of our own experience, to our inestimable loss.

Take for another example the impact of Darwin's metaphor: All life is like a plant which grows in certain prescribed stages from seed to maturation. Widespread acceptance of this biological metaphor is still sending us looking religiously in all directions for stages of development, and wonderfully, how many we have found! We now understand nearly everything human as having stages. That is the strength of the biological metaphor.

However, this metaphor precipitated a myth of all human history, not like a plant in some very important ways, but *as* a single plant in all ways. The defect here shows as a bias, a blind bias, against non-Western peoples and against all history. The myth of progress by definition exalted European and American peoples and derogated others, all those "beneath" or "behind" our advanced selves. Further, the myth of progress produced what Adams calls temporal provincialism. Everything in our "advanced" time is by definition better than anything old; therefore, whatever is "old" is derogated.

Ironically, the myth of progress has been substantially broken by our terrible disillusionment. The horror of the World Wars, the threat of nuclear annihilation, the ecological imbalances we have created, and so on— These things have hardly demonstrated Western or contemporary "superiority!" Yet because we still partly believe this myth, some Unitarian Universalists, for example, almost get hysterical when anyone affirms the value of anything centuries old. But a myth, uncritically accepted as totally encompassing *all* reality blinds us to some reality, to our inestimable loss.

Finally, take for example the impact of my family and subculture's domestic metaphor. In their culture the figure of Jesus Christ is a live, imaginative personification of something very real. That something real is imaginatively bodied forth in their art; it is not imaginary. The myth of Christ re-presents the redeeming power of costing love, ultimately, the most important feature of reality human beings can ever know.

Philosophically, or metaphysically, the deification of Jesus has to be understood as an ontic assertion: The universe *always* includes the redeeming power of love: It never has been, it is not now, it never will be devoid of that power. Whatever other destructive forces may contend against the redeeming power of costing love, these can never utterly prevail. Mythically, that assertion is made with the story of the Son who has existed from before the foundation of the world and who shall reign with the Father, world without end. Existentially, the metaphor opens up wide vistas. It reveals the significance and richness of personal love, to be found and exercised *anywhere* and anchors it in the very structure of being.

However, this myth, too, has its built-in defect. The representation of that power in the exclusive forms of the male father/son relationship — a metaphor drawn from personal domestic life — strongly tends to restrict attention to personal and domestic or interpersonal relationships. Piety tends toward piet-*ism*. Believers become ahistorical. Their religion becomes something concerning individuals and God within the forms of male-dominated, intimate community *only*, and having nothing to do with larger social structures. Because these fall outside the range of the metaphor, the people are simply blind to structures of economic exploitation, racism, nationalism, sexism, etc., to our inestimable loss.

Ironically, adherents of the myth of progress — who conceive themselves to be far in "advance" of fundamentalists — may be equally pietistic. For according to the myth of progress, the circumstances — or social developments — by which people escape poverty, are a matter of "evolution." The poor are poor, not because of particular social structures which we ought urgently to work to change, but because they just haven't sufficiently "evolved" yet. Providence will see that they "evolve" in *slow* stages of maturation. Therefore, the "progressively" faithful rich may conservatively stick to "religion" and avoid "social action." Their pietism is justified by their myth of the world in the same manner as is that of the fundamentalists.

I hope that with this first chapter I have been able to show you why I find the subject of our myths not only intriguing, but important. And why I hope you will read on.

Notes

1. This is an autobiographical essay. I hardly mean to say in what follows that the Reformation began in the 17th century. I assume it began for *my* English-speaking ancestors in the 17th century.

   If you know little of the religious roots of political radicalism and would like to learn, I suggest Roland H. Bainton, *The Reformation of the Sixteenth Century*, Beacon Press, 1952; George H. Williams, *The Radical Reformation*, Westminster Press, 1962.

2. Mircea Eliade, *The Myth of the Eternal Return or, Cosmos and History*, Princeton University Press, 1954.

3. Rudolf Otto, *The Idea of the Holy: An Inquiry into the Non-Rational Factor in the Idea of the Divine and Its Relation to the Rational*, Oxford University Press, 1923. Clifford Geertz, "Religion As a Cultural System" in *Anthropological Approach to Religion*, edited by Michael Banton, Tavistock Press, 1966.

4. The inescapably mythical character of human thought is everywhere discussed and illustrated in, e.g., Tillich's work. See the Index and look up "myth" and (a misnamed project) "demythologization" in the three Volumes of Paul Tillich, *Systematic Theology*, University of Chicago Press, 1951, 1957 and 1963.

   For an amusing account of how a newly contrived myth, that of Freud's "totemic banquet," became "one of the minor gospels of three generations of the Western intelligentsia," see Mircea Eliade, "Cultural Fashions and the History of Religions" in *The History of Religions: Essays in the Problem of Understanding*, edited by Joseph M. Kitagawa, University of Chicago Press, 1967, reprinted in Mircea Eliade, *Symbolism, the Sacred & the Arts*, edited by Diane Apostolos-Cappadona, Crossroad Publishing Company, 1985.

5. More technically, the question is hermeneutical: How do we interpret myths? See Hans-Georg Gadamer, *Truth and Method*, Seabury Press, English translation 1975; or David Tracy's "Chapter 3: The Classic" in his *The Analogical Imagination: Christian Theology and the Culture of Pluralism*, Crossroad Publishing Company, 1981.

6. Friedrich Nietzsche, *The Birth of Tragedy* and *The Genealogy of Morals*, translated by Francis Golffing, Doubleday & Company, Inc., 1956.

7. Paul Ricoeur, *The Symbolism of Evil*, Beacon Press, 1967; *The Philosophy of Paul Ricoeur*, edited by Charles E. Reagan & David Stewart, Beacon Press, 1978; and *Lectures on Ideology and Utopia*, Columbia University Press, 1986.

8. James Luther Adams, "Natural Religion and the 'Myth' of the Eighteenth Century," *Harvard Divinity School Bulletin*, XVI, 1951, reprinted in *The Prophethood of All Believers*, edited by George K. Beach, Beacon Press, 1986; "Congregational Polity and Covenant," lecture delivered at the Meadville/ Lombard Theological School, January, 1977, transcribed by Alice Blair Wesley (available upon request); "The Uses of Analogy in Religious Thought," *Proceedings of the IXth Congress for the History of Religions*, Tokyo: Maruzen, 1960 and to be published in the second forthcoming volume of selected essays edited by George K. Beach.

2

In and Out of the Transcendent Realm of the Imagination and Back in the Mundane with a Difference

I begin here by saying something I already said. I have titled these essays *Myths of Time and History*. I might have called them "A Rational Defense and Critique of the Religious Imagination: Or, How Human Beings Use Wonderfully Imaginative Stories to Inform Ourselves About and Deal With Reality." I fear some might find my attempt to change the way you understand imaginative stories — or myths — drastic.

The understanding of myths presented here does not seem to me to be "drastic." Rather, I see myself as trying to proclaim and explain traditional liberality for a new day, or a traditionally broad and free, though rationally rigorous, way of handling our religious heritage with integrity.

I think I know, and even respect, the reason some Unitarian Universalist hackles rise as soon as anybody raises the subject of our heritage, or our spiritual inheritance. It is because the very meaning of our lives is posited, or expressed, in the myths we hold valid. This is the *freight* myths carry, a precious freight, indeed. Any of us, then, whatever our myths, is apt to react angrily if it looks to us like someone is out to de-rail that freight.

Various groups of religious liberals, holding different myths, are especially wary of any claim to validity for Judaic

Christian myths.

(A parenthetical note on my use of the adjective Judaic. I've never liked "Judaeo," a 19th century neologism of uncertain provenance. It reminds me of "pseudo." I'm glad to see its use diminishing. I've read that even liberal Jews have never liked the phrase Judaeo Christian, a would-be liberal turn of phrase meant to be inclusive, but whose condescension Jews felt. It indicated a reading of common history — yes — but one which all too often subsumed the "Judaeo" part in something — to Jewish sensibilities — not Jewish but Christian. Unitarian Universalists ought to understand that. Unitarians for 400 years have read Christian history as — far too often — a distortion, or even a perversion, of what the Jews gave to us. Some say we ought simply to speak of our Jewish heritage. But that adjective has national and genetic connotations. So I use Judaic. I mean by it: that portion of our heritage stemming from the Hebrew Writings. Similarly, I mean by Christian: that portion of our heritage stemming from the Apostolic Writings.)

Among Unitarian Universalists wary of our Judaic Christian heritage are some we might call our Progressivists. These, holding to the myth of progress and invested in the superiority of the newest and the latest, especially the latest science, hear in any defense of the past a kind of assault on all they hold most dear — as though *new* good cannot be sufficiently valued if *old* good is also valued.

Others wary of our Judaic Christian heritage we might call our World Religionists. These hold to a story — or myth — of the world in which it is prophesied that one day there shall be only one religion, a kind of *potpourri* of many traditions. These hear in any defense of our Judaic Christian myths a reversion to exclusivism — as though *others'* traditions cannot be valued generally if our own *particular* tradition is valued.

Still others, some Women's Liberationists, have become heavily invested in ancient goddess myths of cultures other than Judaic or Christian. These hear in any defense of our heritage an unwitting, or witless, defense of the mythic roots of female oppression. These are impatient of hearing that liberals may arguably read our Judaic Christian tradition as witnessing against, and engendering reform of, every sort of oppression, including female oppression, even female oppression attested in the tradition, itself.

Yet others, those I might name our Stoics, hold to a story — or myth — of an ultimately meaningless universe. For these the meaningless universe is a kind of negative source of meaning. In the Stoics' story the human vocation is to live with whatever fleeting, temporary meaning we can create despite, or in spite of, *against* a negative background of ultimate absurdity. These hear in any defense of our world-affirming heritage a threat to the ontological basis of their defiant stance.

Actually, with time to make qualifications, I would happily call myself a Progressivist, a World Religionist and, certainly, a Women's Liberationist. And yet, here I am planning in Chapter 3 to talk about the myth of the Exodus, in Chapter 4 to set forth William Ellery Channing's Unitarian Christian theology of history, and in Chapter 5 to take up the story — one I think should be a myth for us — of Pastor John Robinson and the Pilgrims. Together these comprise a fairly intense engagement with what I deem to be an authentic and fruitful understanding of our Judaic Christian past, which I earnestly hope will enrich our present and fire our future.

But surely you understand why I'm a little nervous about concentrating so on our past, and why I decided to try to finesse some flak. I hope to show you in this, Chapter 2, that though I am a Unitarian Universalist traditionalist, I am hardly mired in traditional-*ism*.

(I don't like any word ending in -*ism*. When I tag a word with the suffix, -*ism*, I mean to be derogatory. I am opposed, e.g., to piet-*ism*, American-*ism*, absolut-*ism*, individual-*ism*, biblic-*ism*, relativ-*ism* . . . even Unitarian Universal-*ism*.)

In this chapter I will deal with a 20th century story. It is *not* a myth, though it could be argued (and I tend to believe) the structure of transformation in this story is a secular variation on the sacred myths of transformation dominant in the culture as these are liberally interpreted. As I shall briefly point out later, it is very like some famous religious stories[1]. In fact some Tennessee fundamentalists in 1986 claimed it *is* a religious story belonging to conspiring "secular humanists," and so they contested in the courts its teaching in the public schools. Fundamentalists would not like my handling of this story.

Nor is it a Unitarian Universalist story, not even by any of the stretches we sometimes make to own authors not quite really ours. There are no references to this story in our hymnal, although it surely is a story most Unitarian Universalists know.

(Our blue hymnal is our most available collection of Unitarian Universalist myths. The hymn lyrics and the readings in the back of the book lift up the various myths affirmed by various groups of us in our century, whether or not the authors ever identified themselves as Unitarian Universalist.)

Speaking of stories most of us know, I once thought of an experiment I'd like some time to perform with Unitarian Universalists, though I've never seriously tried to talk any into doing it with me. I would need about 100 of us, although 200 or 300 would be better, for several weeks. I would like to conduct a kind of census of the population of the Unitarian Universalist imagination.

My notion is that with a few weeks to work together, and assuming our group of 100-300 to be representative, we could construct two lists of characters known to at least 75% of all Unitarian Universalists. On list #1 we could put the names of characters at least 75% of us have seen bodily, touched or heard directly with our senses. The characters on list #1 could be living or dead, just so 75% of us had ever, even once, actually seen, touched or heard them. On list #2 we could put the names of characters at least 75% of us are familiar with, but only through stories we have heard, read, or seen in pictures, e.g, on a movie or TV screen. The characters on list #2 could be living or dead, historical or fictional.

Think a minute about these two lists. Together they would reflect a census of our *common*, our *shared* Unitarian Universalist mind. List #1 would be very short. In fact it's rather hard to think of any names we could put on list #1. Take Ronald Reagan, for example. A few of us have actually seen and heard him; perhaps a few have even touched him. But not 75%. Most of us only know of him through reporters' stories. He would have to go on list #2. Maybe we could put on list #1 the names Gene Pickett, Sandra Caron, Bill Schulz and Natalie Gulbrandsen. But then maybe not. I don't know whether 75% of just any group 200 or 300 UUs we might gather, anywhere but at a General Assembly, have actually seen, heard or touched our recent and present leaders, or not. It might be that even Gene Pickett, Sandra Caron, Bill Schulz and Natalie Gulbrandsen are mostly known to us through stories!

But think of the length of list #2! Remember, on list #2 we could put the names of any character, living or dead, historical or fictional, just so she or he is familiar — that is: known through stories — to 75% of us. It is easy just to start reeling off names we could put on list #2: Martha Washington, Hitler, Hamlet, the Grinch, Hawkeye and Hotlips, Cinderella's fairy godmother, Lassie, Moses, St. Peter, God.

Surely my thesis is self-evidently correct. List #1, of characters known to the *common* mind of the Unitarian Universalist community, known empirically, through the senses — that is: bodily — would be very short. List #2, of characters known to our community through the use of our imagination — that is: spiritually — would be very long, indeed. Moreover, I would bet on the accuracy of a prediction regarding list #2.

Far more of the characters would be historical than living, and far more fictional than factual.

Now, do this, please. Change the shape of the image we've been using. Instead of thinking of two lists, one short and one very long, think of two circles, a small circle inside a much larger circle, both having the same center. Inside the small circle put the names from list #1. In the much larger circle put the names from list #2.

Now, make another change in the image. Use your eraser. The perimeter around the larger circle might seem to indicate a *limit* to the number of characters we can imagine. There is no such limit. So, in your mind's eye leave the names written there, but erase the limiting perimeter. The perimeter around the smaller circle might suggest a precisely defined *boundary* separating factual from imaginatively known characters. They are not so sharply separable. So, in your mind's eye leave the names written in the smaller circle, but erase the boundary between it and the larger circle.

Have you got that figure in mind? If so, I now declare that you have a representation of what liberals of other eras have meant when they spoke classically, of the different realms of body and spirit; or of matter and spirit; or of nature and culture; or of the small, mundane and temporal realm as distinct from the inexhaustible and unseen transcendent realm of the imagination, which *includes* the world of our senses and also vastly *exceeds* the smaller realm. For the transcendent realm is measureless, un-finite.

The two realms are *not* independent, but mutually interdependent. The transcendent realm, known only through the imagination, is always in some sense controlled and limited by the bodily or material realm. It has to be; it must be. Indeed, if it doesn't sound as though the two are realistically related in someone's speech — when a person starts talking about hearing disembodied voices or seeing ghosts or reading a crystal ball, talking about experience in a transcendent realm independent of the bodily realm *as it is* commonly experienced — we rightly wonder if they may be crazy, insane. Sometimes they are! Maybe dangerously so!

All the same, it's a kind of unrealistic craziness not to acknowledge the reality and importance of the transcendent realm, or to claim that anything we humans know only through the use of our imagination has either no reality, or only some kind of "secondary," derivative reality. What we experience and learn and know of the transcendent realm cuts through and across *all* our perceptions of material, bodily reality, for good or ill, all the time. What we experience and learn and know of the transcendent realm — very much — effects what we are *able* or *unable* to see, hear and touch in the mundane world.

I have called this chapter, "In and Out of the Transcendent Realm of the Imagination and Back in the Mundane with a Difference." With this title I'm trying to say something I think is terribly important, and I can think of no better way to put it, but that whole string of words is something of a misnomer. A "realm" is spatial, and I'm not talking about anything spatial. Further, although we *do* easily — and *must* make very fine distinctions between the transcendent and mundane "realms" all the time — every day of our lives — as the shelves and shelves of books in the world's libraries on the philosophy of language testify, there is no easy way to show how we ever make these distinctions, much less communicate them. That's why we needed to erase the boundary separating the smaller and larger circles in our "figure," to make it a more accurate representation, although a figure with no boundaries is hardly still a figure!

With the rest of this essay I shall try to *show* you what I mean by its title by dealing with a story, known to all of us, about a little girl named Dorothy.

• • •

Frank Baum's marvelous fairy tale, *The Wizard of Oz*, was first published in 1900. My children have grown up with the story. By age nineteen the younger one had read the book three times and seen the movie at least a dozen times.

I can't resist putting in here that Baum published two other books before *The Wizard of Oz,* one on the breeding of chickens and another titled *The Art of Decorating Dry Goods Windows.* Baum's would seem an odd combination of concerns. But on second thought, no odder than the combinations you and I take up. Nor any odder, for than matter, than the queer assemblage of issues to be faced and integrated by any ordinary little girl.

As the book opens, Dorothy is at home on the Kansas prairie. Yet, in a scant two pages we learn that Dorothy could not really be at home in such a setting.

You may never have lived on a dry prairie. I have. But I dare say all of us have at times — maybe very recently — found ourselves figuratively in such a place, in the only home we can claim, but no fit place for the child in us to grow and blossom.

Where the land is very flat, the horizons are very far. On a dry prairie you can see a long way into the distance. But there is nothing lovely or challenging or even interesting in all that space to see, unless the sky is perchance blue. Above a prairie the blue sky can be full of crazy clouds, the sky like an immense blue bowl turned upside down over the plate of earth, the sky as varied at different hours of the day as any ocean. But if the sky is gray, as it sometimes is for months on the Texas Gulf Coast prairie where I have lived, the whole world is gray.

In Dorothy's case the house was cramped, too small, without either attic or cellar to serve as laboratory for a child's imagination. The people in the house were cramped, too. Auntie Em and Uncle Henry, the elderly couple with whom the child lived, seldom spoke. They never laughed. They were withdrawn, irritable, worn out. It can be so, too, with us on our dry prairie.

But the oddest feature of a prairie is this. The grayness of the sky may be more than extended drabness. It may be ominous. For especially during certain seasons, the flat prairie is a dangerous place. Great storms — twisters, tornadoes — may blow up, bringing sudden terror and destruction with the speed of a great roaring train.

A terrible, deadening boredom *and* a terrible, horrifying awareness of looming danger, both of which one is utterly powerless to change: Are not these the dominant experience of many an intelligent child who is at home but not at home in this world? The mundane world as it is, is wholly unacceptable, unaffirmable. At the same time this world, the only one known, may be destroyed momentarily in an eruption of irrational violence. The child is lonely — inexpressibly lonely — afraid, misunderstood *by* others and without understanding *of* others who seem as irrationally mysterious and strange as the threatening sky.

Something must be changed. A great deal must be changed if this child is to grow up healthy, not warped, brave not cowed, able to enjoy the world and also able to confront and construct *at home.*

But the world cannot be changed, not by the child, certainly not yet, not in this condition. It's the alienated child who *must be* transformed. This human situation requires transformation. How is transformation to be accomplished?

Enter: the transcendent realm of the tale, of secret knowledge, of wonder, courage and mysterious help. Thank God! for tales. For through them many hazards of the pilgrimage may be magically negotiated, from a bored and frightened childishness to a vigorous and sparkling maturity.

> This queer cosmic town, with its many two-legged citizens, with its monstrous and ancient lamps, may yet give us at once the

> fascination of a *strange* town and the comfort
> and honour of being our *own* town. [G. K.
> Chesterton][2]

The tornado comes. It picks Dorothy up. It picks up her whole little house, with her and her dog Toto in it, and after a while sets them down in the land of the Munchkins.

The houses of the Munchkins were odd-looking dwellings, "for each was round, with a big dome for a roof." Those alert to the ways of symbol will already take some comfort. Here in this land, so different from home, the vast dome of the sky has been incorporated into domestic architecture. Here the dome shelters.

The first thing validated in the fairy tale is the normal response to strangeness. *Of course* Dorothy was shocked and amazed at all she saw when lifted off her accustomed plain. Indeed, all of us would be gasping with surprise much more often than not if always we were as awake as one must be in fairyland.

> The ... fairy tale makes the heroine a normal human girl; it is her adventures that are startling; they startle her because she is normal.... The fairy tale discusses what a sane [person] will do in a mad world.

This is the great difference which distinguishes the fairy tale from a sober, realistic novel which discusses "what an essential lunatic will do in a dull world."

The whole point of the fairy tale, however, is that the mundane world is *not* dull, anything but! Nor is one generally helpless in face of its madness. The mundane world is dull only to the un-transformed! In the words of G.K. Chesterton, "It is one thing to describe [in a fairy tale] an interview with a gorgon or a griffin [or a Munchkin or a witch or a Wizard], a creature who does not exist." It is another thing, the aim of the tale, to render the reader able to *see*, with imaginative eyes, rhinoceroses, e.g., which do exist though they look as if they didn't.

> One searches for truth, but it may be that one pursues instinctively the more extraordinary truths.

The thing is to get us to *see* the extraordinary truths of the ordinary world! One of the more extraordinary of all extraordinary truths is that very human capacity for transformation. Along with Dorothy in Munchkinland, we begin at once to learn extraordinary truths.

The first she learned was that, completely without her intention, "an innocent, harmless little girl" might be part of an event which destroyed evil and caused other innocents to rejoice, as happened when her house fell on the Wicked Witch of the East. (The opposite can equally well be so; she might have been part of an event that abetted evil and caused innocents to suffer.) And "Who me?" was her normal, astonished response to this extraordinary fact.

Next, Dorothy heard the extraordinarily calm admission of the Good Witch of the South that goodness is not always as powerful as wickedness. Says Chesterton,

> The goodness of the fairy tale is not affected by the fact that there *might* be more dragons than princesses; it [is simply] good to be in a fairy tale.

Amazingly, whatever the relative power of good and evil in our own lives, we all know that it is simply good to be in and of the story when we can be induced, by a tale of the transcendent or through any other agency, to perceive the world beyond our everyday horizons.

But then, having hardly entered this fascinating world of Munchkins, Dorothy learns a third extraordinary truth. She soon knows that as a normal human being, what she *really* wants is to get home.

To get home. How does one get to be at home?

To get home she will have to go on a perilous journey, a pilgrimage, a search for help. One *has to go* on a journey to get home. The "journey" is a spatial image of spiritual transformation from unacceptably weak and fearful to strong and courageous personhood. The journey will, of course, summon up and exercise and strengthen the qualities and abilities of her own true self, but at this point these are yet only latent in Dorothy. She has yet to discover them.

Does the knowledge, that one must be transformed, or go on a journey to get home, always come as a revelation? Maybe so. Such knowledge usually comes as a revelation in fairy tales, anyway, maybe because that's the way it always comes.

> "I'm afraid, my dear," [said the Good Witch of the South], "that you will have to leave us."
>
> Dorothy began to sob, at this, for she felt lonely among all these strange people. Her tears seemed to grieve the kind-hearted Munchkins, for they immediately took out their handkerchiefs and began to weep also. As for the little old woman, [the Good Witch of the South], she took off her cap and balanced the point on the end of her nose, while she counted "one, two, three" in a solemn voice. At once the cap changed to a slate, on which was written in big, white chalk marks:
>
> "LET DOROTHY GO TO THE CITY OF EMERALDS."

> The little old woman took the slate from her nose, and having read the words on it, asked,
>
> "Is your name Dorothy, my dear?"
>
> "Yes," answered the child drying her tears.
>
> "Then you must go to the City of Emeralds. Perhaps Oz will help you."
>
> "Where is this City?" asked Dorothy.
>
> "It is exactly in the center of the country, and is ruled by Oz, the Great Wizard..."
>
> "How can I get there?' asked Dorothy.
>
> "You must walk. It is a long journey, through a country that is sometimes pleasant and sometimes dark and terrible. However, I will use all the magic arts I know of to keep you from harm."[3]

The Good Witch marks Dorothy's forehead with a kiss. The charm will not ensure against all dangers, but it will work against some. So Dorothy sets out, alone.

Fourth extraordinary truth: Once she set out, she "did not feel nearly as bad as you might think a little girl would who had been suddenly whisked away from her own country and set down in the midst of a strange land."

I have been quoting both from Baum's *Wizard of Oz* and from a delightful chapter in one of G. K. Chesterton's books, titled "The Ethics of Elfland." In Elfland, if we are extraordinarily blessed, we may learn quickly what Chesterton calls "the whole spirit of its law," that

> There *are* certain sequences or developments (cases of one thing following another) which are, in the true sense of the word reasonable... necessary [laws of the spirit].

For example, one law of the spirit we may learn from Dorothy's journey is that compassion — simple, utterly spontaneous, automatically self-giving compassion — must precede any real friendship.

In the midst of her own troubles, Dorothy's compassion for the brainless Scarecrow, the heartless Tin Man and the wonderful Cowardly Lion, makes their friendship possible. Her compassion for each of them is quickly reciprocated. They feel as much sympathy for her as she for them. Each is not only prepared to join Dorothy in her search for the way home. Each one, his deficiency notwithstanding, will sooner or later offer essential strength to their enterprise. Compassion must be the starting point of truly cooperative friendship.

A second law of the spirit: Humility must precede any real transcendence of deficiency.

Neither the Scarecrow nor the Tin Man has any false pride. Both readily confess and lament scarcity of mind and heart. Indeed, the Tin Man is so conscious of his mechanical, rusty heartlessness that he knows he must — and so he does — take great care not to hurt others carelessly. True, we only find out about the Lion's cowardice when his bluff is called. But having been shown for what he is, though, the Lion henceforward humbly lets his new friends see whenever he is trembling.

Similarly, Dorothy humbly admits that, although she knows she *must* make her journey, she hasn't the faintest idea where she is going nor how she is to get there. Humility, though, in the story, as truly always, precedes lasting accomplishment.

The four friends face on their journey strange obstacles. They meet wicked witches who unaccountably wish to enslave and oppress both people and animals. They walk near trees which unaccountably reach out and grab passersby. Wolves, bees, flying monkeys, fields of flowers that poison, raging rivers, high walls: All these and others are out to stop, prevent, deter, hurt, even kill our friends.

However, from the perspective of fairyland — where all oddities are simply accepted as part of the story — their obstacles are not a whit odder than ours. What could be odder than these things?

> *Good* people in families assaulted by tension and misunderstanding, economic difficulties, drug addiction, illnesses of every variety;
>
> TV preachers in our allegedly sophisticated time who render the simple, though extraordinary truths of other stories — or myths — into justifications for nationalism and chauvinism;
>
> A President of the most powerful country in the world so frightened by a few thousand peasant socialists in the poorest countries of the hemisphere, in Latin America, that he frequently speaks as though he believes the Washington Monument may be under siege by dreadful conquering hordes day after tomorrow.

Under similarly odd circumstances, Dorothy and all potential victors in fairyland simply accept the oddest reality of all: Evil must be confronted. One must try to overcome it if one is ever to be transformed, to get home, to be a fully functioning, normal human being at home in the world.

Dorothy is assigned, *commanded* to go and destroy the Wicked Witch of the West. I am glad Western author Baum did not, as he easily could have, reverse the direction of his symbolism here and make the Wicked Witch "of the East." No. Dorothy, of the West, had to overcome the Witch of the West.

"But - but - but," Dorothy sputters to the Wizard when she at last wins an audience with the awesome ruler.

Why me? I am only a little girl! How can I defeat the powers of evil? I have no magic powers. I am weak. I have only these simple, inadequate friends, without many brains, with too little heart, without sufficient courage. Why me?

Go. Do it. This is the word of the Wizard.

Whatever would make anyone suppose an ordinary little girl named Dorothy could be transformed into such a victor? Why not? How would this change be any stranger, for example, than that eggs should turn into chickens, blossoms to fruit, or seeds into tomatos?

But these transformations — the stodgy disbelievers in miracles would say — are automatic processes of Nature. Here Chesterton is eloquent.

> ... fairy tales founded in me two convictions: first, that this world is a wild and startling place, which *might have been* quite different, but which *is* quite delightful; second, that before this wildness and delight one may as well be modest and submit to the queerest limitations of so queer a kindness.

> ... the mere repetition [of Nature in the mundane world] made things to me rather more weird than more rational. It was as if, having seen a curiously shaped nose in the street and dismissed it as an accident, I had then seen six other noses of the same astonishing shape. I should have fancied for a moment that it must be some local secret society. So one elephant having a trunk was odd; but all elephants having trunks looked like a plot... The grass

seemed signalling to me with all its fingers at once; the crowded stars seemed bent upon being understood. The sun should make me *see* him if he rose a thousand times...

[As for *automatic* repetition], it *might* be true that the sun rises regularly because he never gets tired of rising. His routine might be due, not to a lifelessness, but a rush of life. The thing I mean can be seen, for instance in children, when they find some game or joke they specially enjoy. A child kicks its legs rhythmically through excess, not absence, of life. Because children have abounding *vitality*... they want things repeated... They always say, 'Do it again'; and the grown-up person does it again until he is nearly dead. For grown-up people are not strong enough to exult in monotony. But perhaps God *is* strong enough... It is possible that God says every morning, 'Do it again' to the sun; and every evening, 'Do it again,' to the moon... It may be that [S/]He has the eternal appetite of infancy... The repetition in Nature may not be a mere recurrence; it may be a theatrical *encore*... It may be that our little tragedy has touched the gods, that they admire it from their starry galleries, and that at the end of every human drama [we are] called again and again before the curtain.

"*Encore! Encore!* Do it again. Be ye transformed," cry the prophets and artists of our religious heritage, who through art would swoop us up with Dorothy into the transcendent world of the imagination, so that we can hear the Word of abundant life. I tell you the message is not very different whether the author is Frank Baum of the *Wizard of Oz*, or Isaiah of the Hebrew Writings, or John of Patmos of the Book of Revelation. John's marvelous Book ends with a fantastic description of none other than "The Emerald City" itself — he calls it the New Jerusalem — where all Creation is eternally and joyously at home.

Be ye transformed. Turn into people who are at home in this amazing world precisely in that you are not spiritually blind to the world's wonders. Be transformed into people whose senses are never dulled so that you don't appreciate the wonder of it all. Enter a covenant of faithful partnership with your heart's allies and be, like Dorothy, ready to *obey* a mysterious mandate to take on and oppose the world's deficiencies and evil, even in the weakness of your own.

Back in the mundane world, we need to ask lots of questions about the particulars of what we are to take on and oppose, so we can do so intelligently not ignorantly. But there's no point in asking *why* we are to oppose evil; it is just mysteriously required of our humanity. The grace of transformation will make you quite as strong as you need to be to run the race set before you, as bright, yourselves, as the racing sun.

The final lessons of Dorothy's story are these.

Help does come sometimes from unexpected sources. One might as well learn to expect unexpected resources to show up any time.

And the most astonishing victories — like Dorothy's over the Wicked Witch of the West in her defense of Toto — The most astonishing victories tend to occur exactly when we have forgot our fears because we have forgot ourselves, and are courageously responding to the abuse of beloved others.

Out of love for Toto, not herself, Dorothy grabs a bucket of water and douses the Wicked Witch. To her amazement, wickedness melts when shown to be "all wet." How many evils in our world might melt if religious liberals now — as many times in the past — should covenant to become a lifelong bucket brigade whose aim is to douse those who threaten our beloved, the precious small and defenseless-against-oppression of every description? The courage to lift the buckets, and win over evil, comes with, and only with, just such bravely self-forgetting affection.

When Baum's story ends, Dorothy is at home on her Kansas prairie. And though Baum does not say so, I would bet all the gold in Munchkinland that she grew up to be a very fine neighbor, parent, church member and County Councilwoman, indeed.

Go thou, let us each one go, and do likewise.

Notes

1. My reason for treating this story, which is *not* a myth, in a book otherwise about myths is precisely the religious importance of transformation through story. My aim is to illustrate that importance, far more amenable to their own worldview than some religious liberals might suppose, while avoiding the resistance of prejudice to be encountered were I to try handling the subject with reference to a traditional myth of salvation.

2. Gilbert K. Chesterton, "The Ethics of Elfland," *Orthodoxy*, Image Books, a division of Doubleday & Co., Inc., by arrangement with Dodd, Mead & Co., 1959.

3. L. Frank Baum, *The Wizard of Oz*, Puffin Books, Penguin Books Ltd., 1982.

3

An Old Story Re-told: Lessons Learned in the Wilderness After Liberation

In Chapter 1, I tried to tell you something of my encounter with Greek religious drama of the 5th and 4th centuries B.C.E. The ancient plays were dramatizations of much more ancient stories, known to the entire population. Several of the extant plays tell the same stories, but with what variations — of character and even plot!

It was those variations that gave me so much trouble with the modernist interpreters of Greek drama. In the handbooks of Greek mythology, the variations were scrupulously listed. "According to author X, Iphigenia, e.g., went here and did this and that; while according to author Y, Iphigenia went there and did thus and so." But then, or so it seemed to me, the modernist interpreters wrote about that whole tremendously varied and fluid body of literature, oral and written, as if they were dealing with something rigid and fixed.

Or, it seemed to me, modernist interpreters projected their own cynicism, particularly onto 4th century Euripides. They read his very free use of his basic material as evidence of the *deterioration* of his religious faith, as though faith *should mean*: swallowing, whole and unaltered by so much as a jot, whatever one has inherited from the past concerning the ways of the gods and humanity. I decided, at some point, that what modernist interpreters made of Euripides' free handling of his inheritance told me more about these interpreters' difficulties in coming to terms with *their* inheritance, than about Euripides'.

Or, to put the focus on me, I was only then, in the 1960s, coming to possess what is called a historical consciousness. How can I summarize, in just a few paragraphs, what is meant by this term, historical consciousness? I'll have a go at it thus; shift with me now to the 19th century of our era.

Attentive readers of the Bible had long been aware of the variations in the stories of the Bible. Now, so long as one assumes that the Bible contains only a purely factual record of what happened in the past — "Nothing but the facts, Ma'am. All we want are the facts" — then a correct understanding of the stories is assumed to call for a "harmonization" of the variations.

Take the four Gospels of Matthew, Mark, Luke and John, for example. The four accounts of Jesus' life and passion vary a lot in their telling, not only of where Jesus went, how long he stayed, what he did in each place, and so on, but also of what he said. It would be fun to know how many hours total have been spent by people arguing over the proper reconciliation of the differences, by people who have wanted an exact itinerary, timetable and transcript.

In the 19th century it began to dawn on liberal biblical scholars: We're missing the points the authors of the Gospels were trying to m*a*ke with their writing, by even trying to "harmonize" these accounts. When people re-tell stories — any stories, but especially stories that have become myths — the telling is altered, consciously or unconsciously, *not* just to be sure their hearers or readers get the facts straight, but to communicate the *meaning* of the story as the teller understands it to speak *to the teller's and the hearers' own time*. Therefore, if we want to understand the artists' variations, the place to look for their meaning is in the changing social context of the artists' times. If we can plausibly reconstruct the artists' situation and times, then we can probably *come closer*[1] to divining what the variations meant, then, and what they might mean to us now.

Slowly, in our century others have come to understand the ramifications of a historical consciousness, discovered by liberal biblical scholars. (In general, it seems to me, secular scholars are terribly chinchy about acknowledging leadership in the realm of ideas as having come from the world of religious scholarship. I know university professors of secular history, literature and political theory who acknowledge no contributions to their own fields, which they use everyday, from the field of biblical and theological studies.) Perhaps I could generalize the ramifications this way.

No living tradition of stories — or myths — of any people whatsoever is to be understood as something rigid and fixed. Even those orthodox and fundamentalists, who *think* they are rigidly adhering to a fixed tradition, are not doing so[2]. Rather, *all* interpretations of, commentary upon, and fresh versions of a tradition — including the orthodox and the fundamentalist — are relative to, or vary according to, their own times.

A living tradition is living insofar as it shapes our minds, institutions and culture. That is to say: Received accounts of the past shape our very perception of what is before our eyes in the present. The past, therefore, also shapes our dread of and/or our hopes for the future.

But further, tradition is *itself* re-shaped in freshly creative ways by the present. Present experience shapes our perception of the past just as much as the past shapes the present. New experience causes us to see the past differently and, therefore, also to envision the future differently. The relationship between the past, present and future in a living tradition is thoroughly and continuously dynamic, changing, becoming. Thus is tradition, not dead, but live. Awareness of the *mutuality* of perception and history, outside which *none* can stand to administer any pure, uninfluenced test, is what is meant by the term historical consciousness.

Historical consciousness radically relativizes all understanding of meaning, or truth claims. It does not at all necessarily imply, however, relativ-*ism*, the claim that there is no basis for any affirmed faith in the meaning or truth of a particular tradition. Rather, a mature historical consciousness makes pressing and simultaneous demands for *integrated* imagination, rationality, humility and courage.

The historically conscious traditionalist says, in effect: Imagine with me what these stories — or myths — of our tradition may have meant in the past or may mean now. I'll re-tell the stories in language of our own times so you can see the meaning I am suggesting we read from them. Is not this interpretation rational? That is: Does it not cohere, or align with and make sense of present experience? There's no way we can absolutely prove any interpretation is correct; so humility is in order, always. Nevertheless, if this interpretation is such that we cannot but believe it is correct — because it makes sense to us — then we're going to have to dare to act on it and from it as we set about shaping the future. Faith, or fidelity to what we cannot but believe is true, requires the courage of our convictions.

That's my introduction for this chapter. As in Chapters 1 and 2, I have begun with an abstract discussion. But I'd rather try to show you what I mean by re-telling a story, in this case the story found in the Book of Exodus of the Torah.

I am ambitious. With my re-telling of the story of the Exodus, specially written for Unitarian Universalists of the 1980s, I would like, at one stroke, to give you a view of what may have actually happened some 3400 - 4000 years ago.[3] (There's no general agreement when, or even whether, Moses lived; plausible arguments vary widely.) I would like to show you, if you did not already know it, how this story is presently being re-interpreted and used with potentially world-changing effect by "Third World" Christians or liberation theologians.[4] And, I would like to give you what may be a fresh view of our own Unitarian Universalist present.

I really believe that if Moses, himself, and his sister Miriam could read my account — who knows? they might — they would laugh with you as you read, and say, "That's it! That's just the way it was!"

• • •

Why Yahweh picked Moses is a puzzler. He stuttered. He had a criminal record. He was 80 years old. He had never lived among the Hebrews. To tell the truth he knew little about them. Surely no Ministerial Search Committee would ever have recommended Moses.

But he was Yahweh's candidate. Yahweh called on Moses to persuade several hundred thousand[5] economic slaves of their promise or, as we Unitarian Universalists would say, of their "inherent worth and dignity." His un-gathered congregation was at the very bottom of the social pyramid. No wonder Moses said, "God! I'm not the one you want to do this!" Some consciousness-raising project he was to take on.

Moses agreed to try, but his misdoubts were prophetic. "Yahweh" means: *I Am What Causes All Things To Come To Be*. Doing as he was bid, Moses went to this mass of slaves and said, "I - I - I Am What Causes All Things to Come to Be has sent me to you." They didn't believe him.

So, Yahweh sent Moses to tell Pharoah to let the people go. Not that he expected that to work in any kind of straightforward way. When has it ever worked to tell the powerful they should stop their unfair use of cheap labor? It does work, though, in a kind of bass-ackwards way, as we see today in South Africa.

Public religious talk about exploitation of the oppressed

angers the powerful. So the powerful try to put the lid on reform-minded preachers. There are various "plagues," at first only annoying — a few "bugs" thrown into the system — but then the disruptions get a little scary. So the powerful clamp down harder. Then there are some fairly serious dislocations. Big profits are threatened and some people die. Yahweh seems to have thought he could pressure Pharoah, with slowly mounting general disorder, until Pharoah should actually throw it all up and say, "Get out, and good riddance!"

That's not the way it worked out.

After severe disorders, Pharoah did finally concede, only to change his mind. He decided this was not a religious problem or a political problem. It was a military problem. So he let the people go as far as the sea and then sent 600 crack charioteers after them.

That's exactly when things got easy, *briefly*. But *nobody* knew it was going to be easy before it was. Confusion is paramount in the narrative. Here were the people on the beach. They could see the chariots coming. It looked like a quick end of their rash venture into liberation theology.

"Holy Moses!" they cried. "There weren't enough graves in Egypt? You had to bring us out here to get us buried? We should have stayed in Egypt. Who minded a little slavery?"

Moses exhorted them, "Stand firm. All you have to do is say no to oppression. God will fight for you."

But Yahweh broke in. "Moses, what in tarnation do you think I can do if they just stand there? Tell the people to *move forward*, and get the lead out!!"

This is the one marvelous part of the story. Yahweh accomplished a technological trick. The sea divided. The people "walked on dry ground through the sea." When they were all on the other side, the sea flowed together. The pursuing cavalry were drowned. In the morning the Hebrews gazed at the dead soldiers washed up on the shore, as the

Filippinos in February, 1986, gazed amazed at all those shoes Imelda Marcos suddenly flew off and left behind.

One day the mighty military and business interests were in control. The next day the mighty had lost control, just like that. One day the people "walked on dry ground through the sea." For a day Moses and Yahweh and the people looked like quite a team. And there was dancing and singing on the other side of the water!

Now a cynic might say, "What's so marvelous about drowning a few hundred soldiers? Why didn't the great God Yahweh just teleport all the masses of poor people to a land of promise?" That's a good question. But then, never did any cynic lead a revolution.

Alas, it wasn't to be so easy out there in the wilderness, even with Yahweh's technological assists.

Moses told the people if they would just pay attention and do what was right, they would never have any problems as serious as the plagues that had come upon the Egyptians.

But then, six weeks later the logistical problems seemed quite serious enough. The people began to say," What are we to eat? At least in Egypt we ate. Moses, you brought us out here to starve to death?"

So again, Yahweh improvised a technological fix, of sorts. He caused the ground to be covered early every morning with a white, flaky stuff.

The people said, "What is it?"

Moses said, "That's your bread."

The people said, "You gotta be kidding!"

It was the world's first fast food. All the people had to do was walk outside their tents, gather it, and eat. On Friday, though, they were supposed to pick up a double order. Yahweh's food service wasn't open on the Sabbath.

These ex-slaves, slow at first to believe they had any God-given promise, soon proved to be quite precocious consumers of divine gifts, and they griped. Some of the folks didn't like picking up their food every darned morning. They tried picking up enough for several days at once. If you've ever tried to eat a day-old Big Mac, you could maybe guess how unsatisfactory that was. Others didn't like the Sabbath shut-down. It ruined the whole weekend. They couldn't stay in and spruce up around the tent, or go off on a side trip, or just sleep in once in a while. No. They must get up early the day before the Sabbath, too, or go without eating for two days.

You can't blame Yahweh for getting a little huffy. He said this people was stiff-necked. *Could* Yahweh have come up with something more to their liking? A menu to match the Hilton's, maybe? That's another good question. Personally, I tend to think he was doing the best he could. At any rate, manna is what Yahweh provided, and so the people ate it. And ate it and ate it.

But then, Moses went off to confer with Yahweh on a mountain top and stayed gone forty days. I've always thought this was the dumbest thing Moses and Yahweh did in the whole story. What would you think if your Minister said she needed to go to 25 Beacon Street for a meeting and then didn't call or write for over a month?

Moses and Yahweh were up there making up the Ten Commandments, of course. But that wouldn't have taken 40 days. What they got totally absorbed in doing, so that they forgot all about the people, was designing their dream church building. They designed a portable church, in pieces, one the people could pack up and move when they moved, and set up wherever they stopped, the perfect church for the mobile society. It was to have elaborate decorations. Moses and Yahweh even drew the embroidery stitches around the hemlines of the priests' robes.

Meanwhile, the people sensibly decided Moses had either vamoosed or been killed. So they got his brother, Aaron, to make them a god. That didn't turn out to be a good idea, at all.

As he later told Moses, Aaron just sort of threw some gold in the fire and out popped this golden idol. There was not much to it. It just happened to be what money would buy, but the people liked it. So, after all those months of wandering around in the wilderness and eating nothing but manna day after day, they threw a party. Some party.

If Yahweh hadn't been so absorbed in his dream church, he might have seen what was developing. But he didn't even look down until the party was in full swing. Then, he got mad!

Moses got mad, too. He stormed into camp and broke some heads. He ground up that golden idol, put it in water and made the people drink it. (Some people think that's what's wrong with our water. We made a god of whatever money would buy, then ground it up and put it in our water. It's probably still not a good idea!)

But then Moses had to go back up on the mountain and try to placate Yahweh. Yahweh first threatened to destroy the people, until Moses reminded him the Egyptians would say the great God Yahweh could lead the people out but couldn't stand them once they were out. Then Yahweh said he would send the people on their way, but he wouldn't go with them. Whereupon Moses said he sure wasn't going any further if Yahweh didn't plan to be with them. He hadn't signed on to do this job by himself!

At length Yahweh did agree to renew his promise freely to go with the people if they would agree to renew their promise to do things the way a free people are supposed to do them. So they entered into a covenant of mutual fidelity, again, and they set out, again, through the wilderness toward the land of promise.

Trouble was, there's much more to the business of being free than the people — or even Yahweh — seemed to know on that night they "walked on dry ground through the sea." That is no doubt why nothing in this story seems to have gone according to anybody's plan, least of all Yahweh's.

But it was time for the congregation's first capital fund drive. Would you believe? They overshot their goal. After the canvass was over, people kept bringing in more late pledge cards. Moses eventually had to ask them please not to give any more for a while. And they, by God, *built* that portable church. Everybody of talent was asked to help, and that turned out to be everybody. This congregation might not know how they ever were going to get where they were going, but they sure had a pretty church. Glory filled it, and they loved it, even if it was in the wilderness.

• • •

I'll tell you what I believe about this myth is true.

In some sense it's a historical story, not fictional. Somewhere, sometime a whole people got hold of a politically religious truth: Ultimately, the God of all creation and history is on human beings' side. And that means: on the side of the many, the oppressed. All people are people of promise, of inherent worth and dignity. And if they don't know it, eventually, Whatever Makes Things Come to Be in history will send them word. To me this is *the* most precious truth in all the world. I don't believe it's true because it's in the Bible. I think it's in the Bible because it's true. It's a lesson of history, still being confirmed today.

Now some might ask — many have asked — "How come the Hebrews got singled out for word of their worth? What about all the rest of the oppressed? Surely they weren't the only poor people 4000 or so years ago."

My answer is: I don't know. I don't know why I, myself, ever do or do not get a good idea. Most of the time, when I get a good idea, I think, "Why didn't I think of this before?" The only answer is: I don't know. The limiting thing about any good idea is that you can't decide to act on it before you have it. I don't even know that the Hebrews were the first ones, or ever the only ones, to have this religiously political idea. It makes sense to me to think we might not have it, except that our culture has inherited this story. Therefore, I treasure this one story above any other or all others in our whole spiritual heritage.

I treasure it, too, for this reason. All political ideas are religious at their root; all religious ideas are political in their implications — whether or not people holding them know so. The great thing about this story is: It is a story — or myth — about people who knew *consciously* that their root ideas were at once religious *and* political.

The Book of Exodus as we have it was only written after the oral traditions of the myth were already hundreds of years old. In still later Books of the Hebrew Scriptures, we are told that again and again, every time Israel got a few fat cats in power, she got the notion that her deliverance from slavery made her special in the sense of *better than* other people; so her power was divinely guaranteed.

That fits my experience. "Special" does *not* mean better. It just means distinct, identifiable, these special — or distinctive — people having had some particular experience others may not have had, *yet*. Other people are also special — or distinctive — they having had particular experience that distinguishes them, too. But how often people distinctively blessed decide they have been blessed because they are better than others! I can understand why the later Prophets sometimes told the Israelites that if they thought themselves special in the sense of better than others, they didn't understand their own story and never had understood it! The same word needs saying, e.g., to super patriot Americans and to elitist Unitarian Universalists.

Many of the elements of the story of Exodus, as it has been handed down to us, seem pretty clearly fictional or requiring figurative imagination. I can do it, but it's hard for me to imagine why that would upset rather than delight anyone, or why the imaginative elements would cause anyone of normal intelligence to miss the points. I lift up what I take to be some of the major points, especially as they may apply to 20th century religious liberals.

Again and again, faith degenerates to a foolish confidence that all reality requires of us is that we say something. Like: We're against oppression and for freedom. Having said that, we really expect God — or The Way Things Come to Be — to do the rest, to work everything out. On the contrary, God Almighty cannot free us if we are not sometimes willing to move forward into unknown seas, against all odds.

When we move forward, against all odds, *sometimes* we do, by God, "walk on dry ground through the sea." Nothing is guaranteed. We're not talking here about superstitious nonsense. Sometimes when we move forward against all odds, we're the ones who get drowned. But then sometimes, all the pieces of a complex situation fall together at the same time and lo! a kind of instant bridge to a new world suddenly appears for those who will cross over, now! Theologians call it a ripe time, a time of *kairos*, a time singularly opportune. Just one more brave, right move on our part, on the part of the whole people. We're not talking here, either, about some kind of Lone Ranger individual-*ism*. Just one more brave, right move on the part of a courageous people, and all kinds of things, that looked impossible or very unlikely, turn out to be a piece of cake.

Our church these days is mostly made up of middle class people. Not many of us have braved a revolution against entrenched government structures on behalf of freedom, although our ancestors did. But there are other kinds of structures it can take a lot of guts to fight your way out of, too. Many of our members have had the experience of walking "on dry ground" from under them. I'm thinking especially about structures of irrational religion and about structures of sexism. Many a Unitarian Universalist, perhaps after much doubt and trepidation, after years of anguish and uncertainty, suddenly one day found it easy just to walk out of whatever it was restricting, diminishing, contorting their lives — only to find—

Not far into new freedom, lack of direction is *almost* as oppressive as whatever it was we left.

Not far into new freedom we still find, technological marvels don't continue to seem marvelous for very long.

Not far into new freedom we still find, whether or not we ever thought so, we need some disciplines we understand and accept freely because we understand their value.

It makes sense to me to speculate, with Martin Buber, that the Sabbath may have been the invention of a religious genius, a great individual leader, the founder of a new religion, Moses. The idea was such a radical departure from the occasional, seasonal religious festivals of surrounding cultures that it seems to bear the mark of a single brilliant mind. Imagine. A *weekly* time for the whole people to seek out the holy, as individuals, yet together! The people didn't understand at first. They may have resisted it for a long time. They seem to have taken it as a rule arbitrarily imposed, rather than a gift. Any discipline must always be received as a gift, to bear fruit in our lives. We miss the fruit completely if we're just "going through the motions" because we think somebody's making us do it.

Not far into freedom, we still find that "whatever gold will buy" cannot provide any kind of workable substitute for what should be our prime loyalty. Especially without freely accepted and fruitful disciplines for seeking the holy, we may decide what we need is more parties. There's not a thing wrong with parties, *per se*. But if we think we can use entertainment to replace sacred meaning, if we think we can fill the center of our lives with good-times, we still find out: It *won't* work. In myths "God's anger" points to something the people learned the hard way, won't work.

But what should be our prime loyalty? Not knowing that, really not knowing, is practically the definition of the wilderness experience. In the wilderness we cry: I know my life is without direction. I know I am drifting. I know my whole family or our whole church or our whole country is drifting, wandering aimlessly. But what is required of us? What does life want from us?

The answer of this great old story: Have you not considered that the conditions of fulfillment might require of you fidelity to that which is genuinely liberating? Look to the political realm. How about looking for meaning in fidelity to those creative forces which actually free people from political poverty, from soul-draining constraint to serve the powerful, those creative forces which make for justice in the world?

You say it's been a while since you personally experienced political liberation? Well, look to the past. How did it go then? Is your memory so short? Have you forgot so quickly? Can you not remember? Look to other people's experience. Can you not imagine it? Look to the future. What kind of world are you hoping for? What would loyalty to your vision of a just world require? You say the voice of justice has not spoken to you lately? Well, then pay attention and w*ait* in faithfulness. If you listen, the voice of justice will call, command and assist, soon enough.

The myth tells us — and I believe — as individuals and as a religious people, we are *first* and centrally to love, with the purity and beauty and intensity of worship, the God of justice in all we do.

Maybe even Moses and Yahweh forgot that. If so, that wasn't the last time religious leaders went off on a pious and private spiritual high of little value to anybody else.

There's lots else to be loyal to, too. Justice is not the only value. But none of the rest will have a fit place in our lives if, as a people, we're trying to put anything else first. We only get ourselves and all we care about in an awful tangle whenever we do.

The good news of the wilderness myth is that forgiveness is possible, whatever our tangle, or whatever pathless place we're in. More than that, forgiveness is necessary. Even Yahweh *has to* forgive, if he wants a people. Forgiveness is: the willingness to let the past be past *and* to enter into a new promise of mutual fidelity, into a re-negotiated and freely re-entered covenant, together.

The good news of the wilderness myth is that wherever the people enter, again, into a covenant of fidelity with the God of justice — no matter how mobile the society, no matter whether God or the people seem to know for sure where they're going— Wherever the people enter into a covenant of fidelity with the God of justice, there will be a church full of glory. They may not know what's out there or how they're ever going to get there. They know to whom they owe their prime fidelity. And that is enough.

It is reassuring, too, to be told that given this clear covenant, the church members' financial resources turn out to be adequate. Or rather, given this clear covenant, the church members turn out to be generous. There is enough money to put up a nice building, buy furnishings, instruments, choir robes and so on, to enhance and help make effective those disciplines of seeking out the holy. I believe this part of the myth, too.

Notes

1. Scholars engaged in biblical criticism long before the 19th century. The term historical consciousness refers to a specific critical concept emerging, in the late 19th century, from long disciplines of biblical criticism.

For an introduction to the history of criticism, see S. J. De Vries, "Biblical Criticism," *The Interpreter's Dictionary of the Bible* Abibgdon Press, 1962; John S. Kselman, S.S., "Modern New Testament Criticism," *The Jerome Biblical Commentary* Prentice Hall, Inc., 1968; Kenneth Hagen, "The History of Scripture in the Church," *The Bible in the Churches: How different Christians interpret the scriptures* Paulist Press, 1985.

If you like to be taught history by a fine novelist, I recommend Chaim Potok's *In the Beginning* Fawcett Publications, Inc. reprinted by arrangement with Alfred A. Knopf, Inc., 1975. This is a story of a brilliant young Jew who must come to terms with the meaning of the biblical and Jewish heritage in the modern world, in face of the challenge of a full-fledged historical consciousness.

2. In Chapter 1, I followed popular usage in referring to my family (and millions of other Southern Americans) as "fundamentalist." The term has come to be applied broadly to any religious people, most recently to Islamic Iranians, e.g., who resist historical criticism whether or not they know there is any such thing to resist. Technically, this broad usage is incorrect.

Technically, fundamentalism names a specific movement, which only developed in the 20th century, in specific opposition to biblical scholarship and Darwinism. It is *not* very traditional, but quite peculiarly modern. For a summary of its 20th century history, see Grant R. Osborne, "Evangelical Interpretation of Scripture," *The Bible in the Churches: How different Christians interpret the scriptures* Paulist Press, 1985.

Not all evangelicals are fundamentalist, by any means. Some consciously regard fundamentalism as a modern heresy. My own religious background might more properly be called evangelical sectarian.

3. See Martin Buber, *Moses: The Revelation and the Cove-*

nant, Harper Torchbooks reprinted by arrangement with Horovitz Publishing Co., Ltd., 1958.

4. I was introduced to Latin American liberation theology by Jose Porfirio Miranda, *Marx and the Bible: A Critique of the Philosophy of Oppression (1492-1979)*, translated by John Eagleson, Orbis Books, 1974; Leonardo Boff, *Jesus Christ Liberator: A Critical Christology for Our Time*, translated by Patrick Hughes, Orbis Books, 1978; and Enrique Dussel, *A History of the Church in Latin America: Colonialism to Liberation* translated by Alan Neely, William B. Eerdmans Publishing Company, 1981.

Other authors on my shelves are Jose Comblin, Gustavio Gutierrez and Juan Luis Segundo.

For an anthology of authors including many others — European, North American and feminist — see *The Bible and Liberation: Political and Social Hermeneutics*, edited by Norman K. Gottwald, Orbis Books, 1983.

5. For an intriguing thesis that the Exodus never occurred as a single, mass event but rather as a slowly spreading, popular religious and political revolution, see Norman K. Gottwald, *The Tribes of Yahweh: A Sociology of the Religion of Liberated Israel, 1250-1050 B.C.E.*, Orbis Books, 1979.

4

A Theology of Time and Character: Classical Unitarian Christian Theology of History

May 5, 1819. It is no exaggeration to say that May 5, 1819, is probably the single most important date in American Unitarian history. On that day William Ellery Channing delivered a sermon in Baltimore, Maryland. He preached before a new congregation in their brand new and grand, but elegantly simple church building. It is hardly conceivable that you and I should be Unitarian Universalists today, but for that sermon.

The sermon was printed and reprinted. Copies sold numbered in the tens of thousands. The ideas in Channing's sermon were not new. On the contrary, they were quite familiar to members of the very large and liberal New England congregationalist churches. But never before had these ideas been so cogently and concisely expressed under the explicit name, Unitarian Christianity.

Directly as a result of this sermon, in the next quarter century some 125 of the original New England parish churches — most of them dating back to the colonial era — changed their name, adding the word Unitarian. And in the next quarter century, another 125 did also. A century later, in 1919, the American Unitarian Association met in general assembly in the Baltimore Church. Delegates installed a large plaque in the Church, on the east wall still, commemorating Channing and the sermon delivered there in 1819, which had given definition and direction to the movement.

Have you ever pondered this irony? Scientists have recently taught us the universe is billions of years old. Ironically, incongruously, we now think a million years is not long, cosmically speaking. Yet we have come to think of the beginning of the American Unitarian movement — a mere century and two-thirds ago — as something that happened in another eon, in a far distant past.

In our time Unitarian Universalists have lost a sense of history. We have lost any immediate sense of connection with our religious forebears, even those of only five or six generations ago. Few of our members have any notion what was in that Baltimore sermon our spiritual ancestors found so fine.

Ironically, the present generations have little sense of connection with the near future, either. Our age is haunted by the fear that ours may be the last age. In short, many in our time have lost faith in history, in the historical meaning of time. Throughout the West, in fact, is a widespread, scandalous conviction, more or less open though seldom bluntly confessed. It is the conviction that human history has no "inherent worth and dignity" nor direction, unless it is toward oblivion.

Or, in the terms I have been using, we might say the transcendent realm of our imagination, or spirit, has been drained of historical elements. We have no story — or myth — of a historical past or future. But then, that is a not quite correct statement, as I shall try to show you. For myths don't just die, even when broken. Parts of them may die even while some of their latent assumptions live on, ghost-like, informing our perceptions as much as ever.

The most stunning evidence of the present absence of a story of the future, among us, is the rather sudden and near total disappearance of a word from our vocabulary, a word that used to be used often in Western, and especially in liberal religious mouths. The word: progress. The word progress has practically vanished from use.

In this chapter I want to try to set the myth of progress in the context of much of Western history. I would first say a little more, though, about the *strange* fact that in our time we have come un-rooted historically.

It is a delusion of our time that the gap — the chasm — between our liberal ancestors and us, has been occasioned by science. Many suppose, "Oh, there's no use studying to learn what our religious ancestors held true because — Well, they were naive. They were not scientifically minded. *We* are scientifically minded."

This is wholly false. In the first place few of us really know much about science. Most of us only know which buttons to push. That doesn't make us scientific sophisticates. Besides, no scientists ever conducted internationally recognized experiments proving the notion that history is not worth studying — or hoping for.

The prevailing assumption — that whatever our ancestors believed should be categorized as trivial, of little or no concern to us now — is a ghostly leftover of the myth of progress, which lives on even though we have given up believing in the future the myth foretold. According to that myth whatever is past has been "surpassed" and is thus "dead," no longer relevant.

However, what occasioned the peculiar loss of faith in history in our time was *not* science, but disappointment, disappointment over how history seems to be turning out. How did this disappointment come to be?

I'm telescoping and simplifying here, but with a broad brush I would paint you this picture of developments and ask whether it makes sense.

A term I will use is Western triumphalism. The term is mythic in the largest sense. It connotes supreme confidence in the outcome or end of the whole story of the human race. *Many* in the West adopted wholesale, a similar story-line of history, a straight-line plot from some significant beginning to the *triumph* of something-or-other. "Something-or-other," whatever it was, having once got started, was supposed to triumph for good some day. That was: triumphalism. The mythic structure of triumphalism remained the same in our culture for some 1500 years.

Augustine usually gets credit for inventing the straight-line plot of the Western triumphalist myth of history.[1] In the 5th century the City of Rome looked as though it might collapse into chaos. There were barbarian invasions, severe economic troubles, and so on. Conservative citizens blamed the new Christians. "The ancient gods of Rome," said they, "are angry at Romans for accepting this newfangled religion!"

But Augustine said no. He said the City of God, at long last, had come down from Heaven to reside in the new church. And working from the church's beginning and out of the church, Christ would gradually conquer all evil in time. Eventual triumph was sure.

Beginning as early as the 12th century,[2] many a Catholic Religious Order, and still later — especially in the 16th and 17th centuries — many a new group of Protestants looked at the Roman Church, after it had changed and grown powerful, and said: The Roman Church is not the City of God come down from Heaven, but its opposite! Now though, at long last, *we* have come to understand the true Christ. *We* are organizing a new beginning, and given *this* beginning, Christ will gradually conquer all evil in time. Eventual triumph is sure.

The Enlightenment *philosophes* of the 18th century despised the Roman Church and Protestants, but theirs too, was a similar, straight-line plot. They said: Religion is but stupid superstition. Now though, at long last, *we* have come to understand that. *We* are organizing a new beginning, a reign of reason, civility and republicanism, and given *this* beginning —

especially now that we have the printing press — education will gradually conquer all evil in time. It will be slow, but eventual triumph is sure.[3]

A variety of Romantics adopted a simpler, but similar plot. American history — including American Unitarian and Universalist history — has a strong strain of Romantic anti-intellectualism running through it. The Romantics have said: Religion is mostly silly superstition; but equally silly is all that fancy reason, civility and education of the Enlightened. These have only been tools of oppressive power. Now though, at long last, *we* have come to understand natural humanity.[4] Just give us land for the simple folk. Given *this* new beginning, without kings, priests, or preachers, without scientists, big government or the elitist reasoning of philosophers, natural humanity — living close to Nature — will gradually conquer evil in time. It will be slow, but triumph is sure.

Orthodox Communists adopted the same straight-line plot. The new beginning was different, namely: Marx's discovery and publication of scientific materialism and the exposure of imperialistic capitalism. Communists said: Given *this* beginning, the class struggle will come to an end; the benign workers of the world will conquer. Triumph is sure.

Westerners have competed and fought fiercely — and fight still — over which of these interpretations of history should prevail. Yet all these, and others, have been triumphalist: linear, straight-line plots from some significant beginning to some triumphant culmination.

In our time, in this century, a tremendous shift has occurred in the Western mind. Throughout Europe and North America people quit ever talking about progress.

> Christians who had hoped
>   for the City of God on earth,
> Rationalists who had looked

>   for one world of science and peace,
> Romantics and Communists who had looked,
>   in different ways, for the reign of natural man:
> All have looked
>   at the World Wars,
>   at the Holocaust and Hiroshima,
>   at the arms race,
>   at the plight of the Third World peoples
>   at Vietnam, at the dangerous ecological imbalances,
>   at the still sorry prevalence of racism and sexism—
> Many looked and decided:
> If this is what we've been moving toward all along,
>   history has no meaning.
> Therefore, there is no omnipotent God.

Now some might protest, "Do we have to bring *God* into this? Not all those people believed in *God*!"

Yes, they did. As Forrester Church, of All Souls Church in New York, keeps telling Unitarian Universalists, "God is not God's name."[5] God is just *a* name for *That Which Makes Things Be and Become.* Everybody has some conception of That Which Makes Things Be and Become, whatever they name it. The question is not: Do people believe in a God, or several Gods? The question is: What *kind* of God(s) do they believe in? What are its powers and values?

Nor is the question: Do people believe in a myth, or in a story incorporating all history? From the kind of history people expect, both their myth and their kind of God can be inferred.

Those *so* disappointed with history, that they quit ever talking about progress, *had* believed, or *wanted* to believe in an *omnipotent* God, whether they named it Christ or Reason or Science or Nature or Education or Economic Determinism or Whatever. Whatever they named it, they ascribed to their omnipotent God power like that of a great machine. And their myth of history was essentially the story of history such as a Great Machine God would turn out. Once a great machine begins to work, it just churns away in accordance with its potent and invariable design. Those with a straight-line, linear myth of history in their heads expected their Great Machine God would just churn out, omnipotently, some kind of successful, machine-made history, from some significant beginning to triumphant culmination.

Ours is a time of mythic confusion. Many liberals despair of any meaning in history.[6] Fundamentalists — of our own and other cultures — wildly call for a spurious "return" to irrational religion. Some feminists want us to resume the prehistoric rites of goddesses worshiped before recorded history began. The mythic confusion of our time may be seen as the aftermath of disappointment. These linear schemes manifestly failed — all of them at once — to materialize in the forecast triumph.

Confusion is not always a bad thing. Confusion may provoke us to explore resources we had too summarily dismissed. Or, to put that another way, if we take it seriously enough, our confusion may challenge and break the assumption that the past has been "surpassed" and again break open the past as a transcendent realm to be mined for genuinely new treasures. We may even emerge from our confusion with a revised and corrected myth of progress.

I suggest: In our time of confusion over the meaning of history, and confusion over the meaning of our own lives in time, we Unitarian Universalists would do well to look again at the system of faith of the generations of Unitarians who began our American movement. William Ellery Channing spoke for them. He set forth their system, with clarity and passion, in the Baltimore sermon on May 5, 1819. It was very far from naive.

Channing very frankly acknowledged both the horror of history,[7] and the ambiguity of all human language making any truth claims about a relative world, a world in which "nothing stands alone," a world in which every word, written or spoken, is a complex continuation of other realities with "infinite connections and dependences," a world requiring — of any who would see the sense of it — a fearfully "great extent of view," indeed, and a fearless commitment to the candid use of reason.[8]

But not only was their faith *not* naive. The faith-full lives, of early generations of American Unitarians, were also extraordinarily fruitful. They bore the fruits of justice in the lives of countless others. With some amendment needed, because ours *is* a different time, I find their faith as radically rational and hope-full as any I know.

I will not deal with Channing's whole argument, but instead recast and re-state the faith Channing laid out, as a theology of history, a theology of time and character. I shall approach the subject in existentialist fashion; that is, through my own experience. I will approach the classical Unitarian Christian faith in history, by telling you an anecdote about myself.

• • •

As you know from Chapter 1, I didn't grow up Unitarian or Universalist. I grew up in a devout fundamentalist family. I was devout myself as a teen.

I had a good friend, George, in high school. George was very bright, brilliant even. He went on to take a doctorate in electrical engineering. He was also a very witty young cynic as a teen.

One day outside our school orchestra room, George confronted me with a riddle, a conundrum: "Can God make a rock so heavy he cannot himself lift it?"

I, being naively devout, was stumped by this no-win logical challenge to God's omnipotence. Yes or no: The power of Almighty God is limited! The riddle is ancient, of course, but I had never heard it or thought of such a thing. George roared with laughter at my confusion.

George and I both converted in our early 20s. From my perspective George is still a cynic. He is now a fundamentalist who fervently believes his omnipotent God is going to send all but a few people to hell. I became a Unitarian. I am still devout but a liberal. I fervently believe the earth's Creator would like to make heaven of earth, but cannot *unless* human beings will freely choose to work with the Divine to make it so. For God is *not* omnipotent.

I at least landed in the right tradition. For in his Baltimore sermon, one of the basic postulates of the system of faith Channing unfolded was: God is not omnipotent; the power of God is limited. Orthodox detractors were appalled. Unitarians drew then, "much reproach."[9] Unitarian principles stirred great apprehension. I would say orthodox fears grew from a refusal to think as hard and honestly as those Unitarians did. But especially from the vantage point of our own time, the system is very interesting.

Today I would transpose the terms of George's ancient riddle, as follows: Can That Which Makes Things Be And Become — Can God make human beings *so* free they may freely choose *not* to do Almighty God's will? Or, put the riddle this way: Has God made free human beings who will not choose to make human history fair and just? even while also making our innate human character such that our own essential longing is *for* the justice of love, which we are by nature able to choose and create, *with* the kind of help God freely offers us?

The question is not a no-win conundrum. The answer is neither yes nor no. The answer of a radically rational faith, which Channing articulated— The answer is: Yes, and yet—

Yes, God has made humanity so free that our freedom is a "heavy rock" *unless* something happens to make the burden light. God ca*nnot* lift history to justice by brute force of Divine will. That would do violence to the God-created freedom of human character. Said Channing, we do not and cannot embrace the Divine as the governing power of our lives "*because* God's will is irresistible." It is not irresistible. We can and do resist God's will, as individuals and societies.

And yet, humanity has been and may be lifted, or raised, in time to ever new historical embodiments of the justice of love *through* the free mutual coursing of Divine and human character. And a glorious lifting it has been and may yet be!

The timeline of history is *not* linear or straight and cannot be. For any lifting to new justice ever requires new and *free* human turning, or repentance,[10] of a great many individuals of character. The lifting requires the turning of a great many away from ignorance and violence, away from the fruitless destruction of injustice — injustice to other people, injustice to the earth itself — toward which we were headed or in which we are engaged as a people, or peoples — the whole race of us.

The lifting requires the *free* turning of a great many, not by force, but with the choice of conscience,[11] toward new fulfillment of newly learned needs for the justice of love. And the needs are always new because our times are always new. The times of humanity are *not like* the uniform products of a some Great Inflexible Machine, though some unchanging truths abide, the same, in all times.

Any historical turning and lifting of a great many toward new justice is always a new uphill struggle. It is always begun by a few, or even one person, of ordinary, yet extraordinary, truly human character. These few are those who, with the integrity of reason and love, are themselves persuaded and who then persuade others of ordinary human character, by word and example, to *see* the truth of what needs be done, changed, created in time. They freely choose to take up the struggle, even rejoice to do so — simply because it is right and because it is our ordinary, yet extraordinary human character, however foolishly we may sometimes deny it, to *want* to do what is right.

The lifting is costly, expensive. The lifting requires ordinary, yet extraordinary courage, patience and sacrifice. It is costly because anytime as a whole people we are engaged in destruction — as in discrimination or exploitation, warfare, or pollution — or even, clearly, headed toward nuclear annihilation of the entire world, always powerful interests profit from the way things are. They will *hold fast* to profits and risk destruction of the very ground they're standing on, rather than yield to reason! Others, without faith, will fear any change, or, without sight, just not see why they should bother.

Though the aim, the fruits of justice sought, is a broad increase of freedom and wellbeing for all, the lifting itself may be, usually is, costly — spiritually, economically and politically. It may even cost blood, life.

You know the costliness of the love of justice, which is— Justice is: the historically-made-real and concrete love of others and their equitable wellbeing.

And yet, human history has been and may be lifted, or raised, in time to ever new historical embodiments of the justice of love through the free mutual coursing of Divine and human character. We have certainly known persons of character engaged with devotion in that costly lifting. We have read of them in the historical records and heard of them, many times. We have seen them with our own eyes. Some of them are among us. Their character is glorious! "By their fruits you know them."

And isn't this true? We are drawn to some of the most effective of these — we love them and enjoy working with them — because even while engaged in trying work, they do all they do with a certain lightheartedness, laughter and the sheerest freedom — of fun!

And from the real history
>of the concrete fruits of *their* lives,

you may rationally infer —
>especially as you compare those fruits
>with what you know is the true longing
>of your *own* ordinary, yet extraordinary mind,
>conscience and heart,

as you feel the inclination, the pull, the lure
>of your own character—

You may infer,

you may *know*
>with all the richness of sufficiency you need
>for a rejoicing, rational faith—

You may know the character
>of that which makes *them* be and become,
>of that which makes the kind of history
>*they* expect and freely work for—

You may know the only God
>of love, reason, justice and freedom,
>whatever the Holy is named,

and holy Hope in and for history.

This God is, and wants and works — with ordinary, yet extraordinary human help — to lift the whole earth and every child of earth.

The generations of Unitarians who began our American Unitarian movement believed they might rationally and gladly commend their souls, eternally, to the hand of the only God, as they together committed themselves to *move* in directions indicated by free and rational inquiry concerning the lure, into a new future, of their own conscience.

They believed further, that in their own ambiguous dialogue concerning what might be right for them to do, from their own mouths, they might yet clearly hear spoken — the Word of God.

The clear implication is: Even the power of Almighty God is limited, restricted to work within the limits of free human character. Given the otherwise unlimited, divine or human, use of all other powers — of all wealth and the arts of science, technology, manufacture, and/or weaponry, howsoever great or combined — nothing, save *the free exercise of human character*, can save any history from the destruction of injustice or give it any ultimate worth or dignity. Instead, given *only* the sufficiently free exercise of ordinary, yet extraordinary human character, all other powers combined shall not stand against, but fall before — love of and faithfulness to the ways of justice. For it is there, in the co-incidence of human love of and fidelity to justice, that the ultimately free character of every human child and Almighty God are the same.

And that is why the care and nurture of the character of *every* individual matters so much. For nothing in heaven or earth is so precious as the human character of even the least of us.

I believe I have accurately re-stated and recast the theology of history, the faith in time and character, of the early generations of American Unitarians. It is summarized in the fourth and fifth lines of James Freeman Clarke's list of Unitarian beliefs, engraved on the front wall of the Baltimore Church: salvation through character; progress onward and upward forever.

What I have followed Channing in calling "this system" of faith, does indeed imply a story — or myth — of time. We need to revise and correct our understanding of the myth of the progress of the race.[12] It is not rightly understood as the story of a mechanical escalator proceeding in a straight line, from any beginning point to upper end. Rather, it is more like the story of a road up a mountain, from whose heights one can see a "great extent of view." It is a story of a winding road upward which God summons us freely to survey, cut and build and then to climb, to the very stars, on our own feet, and not alone and not away from, but together with the whole earth.

More needs to be included in any description of early 19th century American Unitarian Christian faith. Let me try to explain it this way.

Without giving rational offense, I am sure, I spoke earlier of persons of ordinary, yet extraordinary character, very real people, who by word and example, have persuaded others — and us — *freely* to move with them in the ways of true character. We have all known them. Without them we are quite capable, as whole peoples, of driving without turning straight to destruction. The movement of history in positive directions depends crucially, truly, on their costly service of love to us all.

The generations of Unitarians who began our American movement understood Jesus — his words, his life and the fidelity of his costly love, unto death — as the example, the pattern *par excellence* of ordinary, yet extraordinary human character. He was, to them, exemplary, a model, a paradigm of what human character, fully unfolded, might become, the perfection of character, and therefore, an inexhaustible resource of instruction and comfort in their own costly struggles.[13]

In their terms, his very human teaching and his very human life was a supernatural revelation. Those terms need not give us rational offense; they can be transposed.

Supernatural simply means: ordinary, yet extraordinary. Channing and many another Unitarian teacher of their generations labored all their lives to proclaim: The extraordinary is but the unfolding of what can reasonably be shown from experience to be implicit in the ordinary.[14] If you cannot by reason show the connections with the ordinary, the extraordinary is *not* extraordinary; it is foolishness! "If religion be the shipwreck of understanding, we cannot stay too far from it!" When we speak, even of the ordinary, yet extraordinary Christ, we are not talking about something foreign or strangely weird, but about what we ordinary, yet extraordinary human beings may do and become, we ordinary daughters and sons of humanity and of God, in history.

A revelation is simply the appearance, to human minds, of an extraordinarily convincing paradigm. A paradigm is: a pattern perceived which *lifts up* to rational view — makes a flowchart presenting, or sheds light on — the orderly ways of a dynamically related whole, or, as we would now say, on "the interdependent web of existence of which we are a part." Or, to use again as in Chapter 1, Paul Ricoeur's term, a mythical paradigm, one revealed in a story, re-presents reality itself.

Like any other paradigm which appears to human minds, it is rationally convincing precisely insofar as it may be tested, by reason, in ever new experience, and repeatedly found to disclose yet more new truth, useful in choosing new direction toward a new and better time.

It was in this sense the generations for whom Channing spoke understood Christ's words: If I be lifted up, I will draw all humanity unto me. I am the truth, the way and the light. My yoke is easy; my burden is light. Take up your cross and follow me. And, truth shall make you free.

But as Channing might say: For heaven's sake do not suppose that when we speak of the appearance to human minds of any such *fruitful* paradigm of ordinary, yet extraordinary human character, we are talking about anything less than the *most* marvelous and holy thing we can ever know! For what is more wonderful in heaven or earth! than the ways of human character and mind in time! For these human ways are also the ways of — not omnipotent, and yet — Almighty God.

Channing had taken as his text a sentence from Paul's letter to the Thessalonians: "Prove all things; hold fast to that which is true." Near the end of his sermon, he said of the faith of the first generations of American Unitarians,

> We have embraced this system not hastily or lightly, but after much deliberation; and we hold it fast not merely because we believe it to be true, but because we regard it as purifying truth ... able to 'work mightily' and to 'bring forth fruit' in them who believe.

May it be said of us, their heirs: The faith we hold fast has also been able to work mightily and to bring forth fruit in us who believe.

Notes

1. Augustine's vision of the glorious end-time had much precedent in Hebrew and Apostolic Writings. The introduction of slow but irreversible gradualism into the schema was his innovation. Augustine, *Concerning the City of God Against the Pagans,* translated by Henry Bettenson, Penguin Books published in Pelican Books, 1972.

2. See a very brief article on Joachim of Fiore by Marjorie Reeves in the section, "The Medieval West," *The Study of Spirituality,* edited by Cheslyn Jones, Geoffrey Wainwright and Edward Yarnold, SJ, Oxford University Press, 1986.

3. For a concise and broad treatment of changing conceptions, over the Western centuries, of coming social structures as related to interpretations of time and the times, see Rosemary Radford Ruether, *The Radical Kingdom: The Western Experience of Messianic Hope, Paulist Press,* 1970; and Paul Tillich, "Historical and Nonhistorical Interpretations of History: A Comparison," *The Protestant Era* (Abridged Edition) translated by James Luther Adams, Phoenix Books, University of Chicago Press, 1948 and 1957.

4. See Daniel Boorstin, *The Lost World of Thomas Jefferson,* Beacon Press, published by arrangement with the author, 1948 (first published in 1948).

5. F. Forrester Church, *Born Again Unitarian Universalism,* Cone-Lewis Printing Co., first deliverd in August, 1981; *Father and Son,* Harper & Row Publishers, 1985.

6. For an excellent short article on 20th century despair, especially in the literary world, see Gordon E. Bigelow, "A Primer of Existentialism," *College English,* December, 1961.

7. "We read with astonishment and horror the history of the church; and sometimes, when we look back on the fires of persecution, and on the zeal of Christians in building up walls of separation, and in giving up one another to perdition, we feel as we were reading

the records of an infernal rather than a heavenly kingdom. . . .sheltering under the name of pious zeal the love of domination, the conceit of infallibility, and the spirit of intolerance, and trampling on [people's] rights under the pretence of saving their souls." *The Works of William E. Channing*, Lenox Hill Publishing & Distributing Co., 1882, reprinted 1970, p. 382.

8. "Now all books and all conversation require in the reader or hearer the constant exercise of reason . . . Human language, you well know, admits various interpretations; and every word and every sentence must be modified and explained according to the subject which is discussed, according to the purposes, feelings, circumstances, and principles of the writer, and according to the genius and idioms of the language which he uses. . . .The word of God bears the stamp of the same hand which we see in his works. It has infinite connections and dependences. Every proposition is linked with others . . . Nothing stands alone. . . .The Christian dispensation is a continuation of the Jewish . . . requiring great extent of view in the reader. Still more, the Bible treats of subjects on which we receive ideas from other sources besides itself, — such subjects as the nature, passions, relation, and duties of [humankind] . . ." Channing, p. 368.

9. ". . .a minister is to be given this day to a religious society whose peculiarities of opinion have drawn upon them much remark, and may I not add, much reproach. Many good minds, . . . I am aware, are apprehensive that the solemnities of this day are to give a degree of influence to principles which they deem injurious. The fears and anxieties of such [minds] I respect; and [believe] they are grounded in part on mistake . . ." Channing, p. 367.

Channing challenged the logic of positing the omnipotence of God. He did this to defend both divine and human character, contesting the orthodox doctrines of absolute divine sovereignty and predestination, and their counterpart, the absence of any human role in salvation. He also answered the related orthodox charge, that the Unitarians made "an unwarrantable use of reason in the interpretation of Scripture." Channing, p. 367.

His defense of God's just and loving character and of human responsibility to use the gift of rationality is phrased more in devotional than philosophical language. (He was, after all, preaching and not giving a dissertation.) Channing was, however, rigorous in his *logically* correct assertion that a God *with* omnipotent power, unrestrained by the divine character, would be a God *without* character. If there is nothing God *cannot* do without contradicting divine nature, then God is characterless. Further, a God who would not freely choose to leave room for the free role of human character, *could not* also choose to create humans who would be anything other than machines. I.e., divine and human freedom each logically imply the other. You can't have a logical concept of one without the other.

Emphasis added in the following passages, to lift up denials of divine omnipotence, is mine as are the words in brackets.

"...God *never* contradicts in one part of Scripture what He teaches in another; and *never* contradicts in revelation what He teaches in his works and providence. Without these principles of interpretation [unless we can posit *inviolable* rationality in the world], we frankly acknowledge that we *cannot* defend the divine authority of the Scriptures. Deny us this latitude, and we *must* abandon this book to its enemies." p. 369.

"...God has *given* us a rational nature, and will call us to account for it. ...We may wish, in our sloth, that God had given us a system demanding no labor of comparing, *limiting*, and inferring [logically]. But such a system would be [impossibly] at variance with the whole character of our present existence [and not any system at all]..." p. 370.

"...if God be infinitely wise [without limit], He *cannot* sport with the understandings of his creatures. [Divine wisdom and the logical *possibility* of accurate human conception each logically imply the other.]

"We believe in the *moral perfection of God* [Channing's emphasis] [not in God's perfectly infinite power]. We consider no part of theology so important as that which treats of God's moral character [as far more important than God's power].

"We conceive that Christians ... have too often felt as if He were raised, by his greatness and sovereignty, above the principles of morality, above those eternal *laws* of equity and rectitude to which all other beings are subjected. ...We believe that his almighty power is *entirely submitted* to his perceptions of rectitude; and this is the [logically necessary] ground of our piety. ...it is *not* because his will is irresistible [which it *cannot* be], but because his will is the perfection of virtue, that we pay him allegiance. We *cannot* [without logically violating our own nature] bow before a being, however great and powerful, who governs *tyrannically.* ...We venerate not the loftiness of God's throne, but the equity and goodness in which it is established." p. 376.

"God's mercy... has a regard to the character as truly as his justice [and so *cannot* be arbitrary, unlimited by human character]." p. 376.

10. "God's mercy... desires strongly the happiness of the guilty; but only through their penitence." p. 376.

11. "We look upon [rationally interpret] this world as a place of education, in which He is training [human beings]... by conflicts of reason and passion, by motives to duty and temptation to sin, by various discipline suited to *free* and moral beings; for union [coincidence] with himself..." p. 377.

"...by [the divine] Spirit we mean a moral, illuminating, and *persuasive* influence, *not* physical, *not* compulsory, *not* involving a necessity of virtue. We *object,* strongly [on logical grounds] to ... ideas of many ... respecting [human] impotence and God's irresistible [omnipotent] agency ... they [illogically and falsely] make [human beings] machines." p. 380.

12. For example, Channing's frequent use of the phrase "the childhood of the race" is indefensible, especially when used, as he did use it, to imply the "immaturity" of Jewish faith. This is one instance— others could be cited — showing that close to a historical consciousness as Channing's rationality brought him, he did not quite achieve it. He fell into the *unnecessary* trap of apologetically motivated pressure to defend his own religion by denigrating what came before it in time. No excellence, of any time, needs that kind of comparison.

13. "We read his history with delight, and learn from it the perfection of our nature. We are particularly touched by his death ... and by that strength of charity which triumphed over his pains. ...we look up to heaven with new desire when we think that, if we follow him here, we shall there see his benignant countenance, and enjoy his friendship forever." p. 381.

14. "We read his history with delight, and learn from it the perfection of our nature." p. 381.

5

The Pilgrims and the Spirit of the Covenant of the Free Church

I like the way this chapter ends. What I have in mind is to work up to a kind of prose poem in praise of the spirit of the covenant of the free church, inspired by a return, in imagination, to the beginning of the free church as we know it, among the 17th century Pilgrims.

Not long ago I had occasion to look up in the dictionary the word likely. I read there, "Likely: If something is natural and easy, it is often likely."

I grinned when I read that. For I am dedicated to our free church which I believe with all my head and heart is utterly natural, meaning: fitting, in all ways. The free church, I believe, in its essential conception and right functioning, fits who we human beings really *are*, what we urgently need and want and can become, and what the world needs of us. But it surely isn't easy. I am even ready to say the thriving free church is in every respect unlikely.

The free church is natural in the way it is natural for a boy or girl to learn ballet or mathematics or farming, and to grow up to be a *fine* artist or scientist or business manager or citizen. But for all the naturalness of these lines of development, there is yet much to frustrate and thwart the unfolding of knowledge and skill. So many factors make a strong, effective and powerful free church unlikely, indeed.

To put the matter bluntly, our free church is not presently nearly thriving enough, not strong enough, not effective or powerful enough. We need an unlikely re-formation.

We need a better appreciation of the role of imaginative story — or myth — in all human culture, including our own.

I can't resist inserting a story here. I think I read it in one of Gregory Bateson's books.

A bright young computer programmer became obsessed with a certain question. She wondered: Will computers ever be able to think and search for truth and make decisions concerning truth on their own as human beings do?

So, she worked long and hard to feed into the computer the data she figured it would need to answer this question, and one day she was ready. She typed the question: Will computers ever be able to think and search for truth and make decisions concerning truth on their own as human beings do? She touched ENTER. The computer whirred and whirred. At length it stopped, and these words appeared on the display screen: Your question reminds me of a story.

The programmer was terribly disappointed. She had looked for a straightforward propositional statement: Yes or no: Computers will, or will not, someday be able to think and search for truth and make decisions concerning truth on their own as human beings do. She got instead reference to a story! But then there was more.

There appeared on the screen these unlikely words: Shall I tell you my story? And there and then was born a new community of two — potentially many more — of as many as might know *or learn* the disciplines of asking and responding *with* the computer. It was a spiritually human community, however alien to things human one of the participants might previously have seemed to the uninitiated.

Most of the time when we regard others as alien, we have

not really heard their story, nor they ours. A quintessential characteristic of humanity is that we tell stories, by definition a social activity, eminently civilizing and community-building. Unitarian Universalists need a rational appreciation of the role of imaginative story — or myth — in all cultures, including our own. That is what I meant in Chapter 1 to say, strongly.

We need to stretch our minds beyond a narrow reaction to the narrowness of fundamentalist or orthodox talk about being "saved," and grasp liberally and freshly the meaning of — the need for and the extraordinary possibilities of — transformation of human minds and hearts. That's what I was saying in Chapter 2.

We also need to learn to transpose — or re-formulate — the terms of our spiritual ancestors so that we can re-connect with centuries of religious experience. That was what I was saying in Chapters 3 and 4.

We need access to the past, especially because we achieve our identity — we learn who we are — in understanding where we have come from as a people. We learn that, through stories of our ancestors, usually called history, not myth. The distinction, however, is not a matter of their differing importance, but of differing methods of research and interpretation appropriate to different genres. A myth is a story freighted with the very meaning of life. A historical story becomes a myth if it is freighted, for us, with the very meaning of life.

But we also need the data of our ancestor's visions, accomplishments *and mistakes*, for the light these throw onto the path we need now to take. The past is like a great bank, a wealth of data, ours for the free exercise of disciplined imagination. Cutting ourselves off from history is like deciding to try to run a business without using the banking system. It can be done, but only on a very small scale, which does *not* fit what the world needs of people of liberal faithfulness.

And we Unitarian Universalists need a new model of the

meaning of free religious community, not to discard our precious emphasis on individuality but to correct a devolution into debilitating individual-*ism.*

If you think a call for such an unlikely re-formation is a tall order, I am undismayed. Everything I've been talking about in these essays has been unlikely. The 16th and 17th century Reformation was unlikely. Frank Baum's having written *The Wizard of Oz* was unlikely. The ancient Israelites' vision of a freely covenanted people was unlikely. The extraordinary fruitfulness and influence of 19th century American Unitarians was unlikely.

All were natural in this sense: Ordinary connections with antecedents and context can be shown. Yet, the turn events took to eventuate in these things was in every case unlikely.

So, I look for signs in our context which may turn out to be antecedents of an unlikely liberal religious re-formation. I find them, signs of hope.

Our re-appropriation in the new Principles and Purposes statement of the word covenant is a hopeful sign.

I see other signs. I attended SUUSI last summer, the Southeast Unitarian Universalist Summer Institute at Radford University in Virginia. For a decade SUUSI has been drawing some 1300 Unitarian Universalists of all ages from all over the Southeast and other parts of the continent. As at Ferry Beach, UUMAC, Star Island, Lake Geneva, SWUUSI — all the places where we gather in the summer — certain traditions have developed at SUUSI, patterns of corporate expression. Because they have proved fulfilling, they are repeated. By a kind of overflow effect, they become more fulfilling.

I was intrigued by the thrust of songs sung at SUUSI by these 1300 UUs, some of them sung over and over, songs about authentic community.

One, titled "Weaving," was written by John Corrado, Minister of our Church in Grosse Pointe, Michigan. The first verse goes like this.

Let us join in human weaving
in blending all the textures of our lives.
Spinning dreams born of believing
a magic pow'r abides.

Weavers of the dreams we share
wishing wishes few would dare
ours a loom where all threads gather
to dress the world with love.

Another by Carole Etzler, sung by the women, calls up those community members of the past who still serve. It is called "Standing Before Us."*

These are the women who throughout the decades
Have led us and helped us to know
Where we have come from and where we are going,
The women who've helped us to grow.

These are the women who joined in the struggle,
Angry and gentle and wise.
These are the women who called us to action,
Who called us to open our eyes.

These are the women who nurtured our spirit,
The ones on whom we could depend.
These are the women who gave us their courage,
Our mentors, our sisters, our friends.

> Standing before us, making us strong
> Lending their wisdom to help us along.
> Sharing a vision, sharing a dream
> Touching our thoughts, touching our lives
> Like a deep-flowing stream.

---

*©: Used by permission. To order music, write to Carole Etzler / P.O. Box 826 / Springfield, VT 05156.

Then there is one by SUUSI participant, Adele Abrahamse. It has almost become the SUUSI anthem. I wish the lyrics were less abstract. But I am struck by what they seem to be reaching for, the covenant.*

> There is something between us that words can't define
> Existing in silence and outside of time.
> Though we just might forget in the passing of days,
> There's still a connection that won't slip away.
>
> I have opened myself to the sound of the lute
> And where once I heard chatter, right now I am mute.
> Rejecting the noise of the usual hours,
> I feel in the stillness this union of ours.
>
>> We're connected through love.
>> We're connected through life.
>> We're connected through stories
>> and tears in the night.
>> We're connected through memories,
>> connected through friends.
>> Feel deep the connection made strong again.

For a host of historical reasons, in our time religious liberals have a vision of world community — dream of it and yearn for it. Yet we have an inadequate understanding of the kind of *local* community that fosters world community. Our local churches and fellowships are mostly small and not notably effective. Our emphasis on individuality has devolved into a debilitating individual-*ism*, the bane of authentically abiding and mighty community.

Modern religious individual-*ism* is a kind of comsumer-ism. People think the church is like a supermarket. "They," should put out attractive products, so I can drop in and pick up

---

*©: *Used by permission. To order music, write to Home Arts Music / P.O. Box 745 / Charlottesville, VA 22902.*

what I need. If "they" don't, I won't buy. "I" need not be bothered with any problems of capital investment, what products to stock, or how to help if there's ill feeling among the personnel. Heaven forbid any should suggest that Membership might *mean* that I will pledge liberally, serve on at least one committee and always attend — as sacred events — Annual Meetings of the Congregation. "I" am only concerned to get what "I" like. If "they" don't provide it, to hell with them. That's consumerism.

Modern, individualistic religious consumerism is only "the latest form of infidelity." It's not all that new. It is but a passive form of individual*ism*, a plague of much longer standing in the whole Protestant tradition, an inability or a refusal to master the skills of *corporate* authenticity. Our ahistoricism — many UUs have little notion how our churches came to be — stems from the same thing: a certain arrogance toward the worth of what any others think, even including those of the past to whom we owe our historical existence. We might overcome uncooperative consumerism and ahistoricism through more knowledge of our history, "overcome history with history."

• • •

Shortly after he resigned as Minister of the Second Church in Boston, Ralph Waldo Emerson wrote in his journal in 1831,

> As fast as we use our own eyes, we quit these parties or unthinking corporations, and join ourselves to God in unpartaken relation.

On another occasion he wrote,

> No facts to me are sacred, none profane; I simply experiment, an endless seeker, with no past at my back. ["The Over-Soul"]

Both those sentences are close to complete nonsense, albeit eloquent nonsense. *Thinking* "corporations" — his family, congregations, schools, publishing and book selling companies, Harvard College — *groups* of dedicated, cooperating people, taught Ralph Waldo Emerson "to use [his] own eyes" and taught him of possible experience of God. Humans are social creatures. We cannot "partake" in anything outside relation with other human beings. And life requires of us discernment of which experiments have worked and which haven't, discernment we continually work out — if we live at all — in cooperative dialogue with the perspectives of others.

Some life! With no need for others' insight or correction! Life as a shopping spree, a casual hunt for what pleases the unfettered "seeker," with no ties to past or future. Impossible!

But the fact is the whole Protestant development and, in particular, Puritan varieties of the Protestant development from which Ralph Waldo Emerson and we derive, have always tended to run off toward excessive individual-*ism*. It's one thing, a wonderfully healthy thing, to take the inherent dignity and worth of every individual so personally to heart that one gains a heightened sense of one's own value. It's another, a kind of selfolatry — a form of idolatry — to say as Emerson did,

> Foolish people ask you . . ."How do you know it is truth, and not an error of your own?" We know truth when we see it, from opinion, as we know when we are awake that we are awake. . . .Ineffable is the union of man and God, in every act of the soul. The simplest person who in his integrity worships God, becomes God. ["The Over-Soul"]

Members of the Second Church of Boston, in 1830, would almost certainly have disputed that statement had their young minister voiced such an utterance in their pulpit. He had to get himself out onto the lecture circuit, away from the disciplines of the "unthinking corporation," before he could say such as that unchallenged.

The word spiritist is a technical name for certain Puritans so sure of their personal communications with God, that they held their opinions to be — not opinions susceptible to error — but directly revealed truth without need of testing, for sense, in the church community. The spiritists — Anne Hutchinson, e.g. — simply dismissed two all-important and related questions: How do you know what you claim to know? And will it stand shared, critical inquiry in the community? "I have prayed and 'become God;' so I just know" was not a reply to those questions which either the corporate-minded Puritans of the Mass Bay Colony or their direct descendants, the great majority of Emerson's fellow Unitarians in the early 19th century, accepted as adequate.

Emerson was an irenic spiritist. He spent his years, after he left his pastorate, quietly penning splendid, if often airy, words. He never used his claim to have "become God," at least from time to time, to justify any wild actions. But plenty of other spiritists did, in the 16th and 17th centuries. In short, those were pretty wild times.

In Chapter 1, by way of telling you about my personal religious background, I began by saying that common, ordinary people in the 17th century got hold of the Bible in their own language. They gained from it a tremendously heightened sense of their own individual worth. They soon deemed themselves worthy, their status as commoners notwithstanding, not only to interpret the Bible for themselves, but also to measure, according to their reading, everything from the local preacher's sermon to the policies of the King.

What was that experience like, that "getting hold of the Bible"? Maybe this: Imagine yourself as Dorothy, living on that dry prairie, and all of a sudden you begin to be transported to Munchkinland several times a week. Heady stuff!

An imagination explosion was begun with unauthorized translations of the Bible, in 16th century England. Along with these translations came the beginning of rowdy challenges to authorized interpretations, which would eventually shake the foundations of every social structure inherited from medieval times.

Thomas Hobbes, looking back on this era, wrote in *Behemoth*,

> After the Bible was translated... every man, nay every boy and wench, that could read English thought they spoke with God Almighty, and understood what he said, when by a certain number of chapters a day they had read the Scriptures once or twice over.[1]

"Every man ... boy and wench" who thought she or he "spoke with God" and "understood what he said" did not, however, agree on what "he" said. In 1588 a Jesuit priest, one William Weston, was in jail in England. From his cell he watched an outdoor Puritan gathering. Wrote Weston,

> Each of them had his own Bible, and sedulously turned the pages and looked up the texts cited by the preachers discussing the passages among themselves to see whether they had quoted them to the point, and accurately, and in harmony with their tenets. Also they would start arguing among themselves about the meaning of the passages from the Scriptures — men, women, boys, girls, rustics, labourers and idiots — and more often than not... it ended in violence and fisticuffs. [This took

> place] on a large level stretch of ground within the precincts of the prison. Here over a thousand of them sometimes assembled, their horses and pack animals burdened with a multitude of Bibles.[2]

If you infer from this account that the various religious groups into which the Puritans split were nearly all a fractious and factious lot, you are correct. Here we see the beginning of the tradition from which American Unitarian Universalists spring.

We can see in this anecdote two aspects of our inheritance, one of which we still proudly claim, the other of which is still somewhat embarrassing. Namely: our fierce insistence on owning and defending our individual views, and the fact that, given this insistence, agreement among us is not always readily forthcoming.

Or, to put that with less understatement, while the whole Protestant development — and in particular the Puritan part of that development — meant new visions of a new world, of enormously creative power, it also carried within it, and carries still, a strong strain toward anarchy. In other words Protestantism *is*, in significant measure: a problem of authority and politics. How do we define the authority of truth, and, on the basis of that authority, how do we organize our communities?

(Parenthetically, apart from the subject of this essay on the spirit of the covenant, it is fascinating to read in histories of the radical left-wing of the Reformation how many in these groups were universalists, finding the doctrine of universal salvation biblical.[3])

In the disruption and confusion and argument of 16th and 17th century England, we find the birthing of both American Unitarian and Universalists' immediate ancestors, as well as those of the Baptists, Presbyterians, Episcopalians and others. Of particular relevance now, I find, is the story of one particular group, the story I would have us acknowledge is our myth.

• • •

In 1607 William Bradford was seventeen years old. He was present at the formation of an unlikely new community, a church that would be known to history as the Pilgrim Church of Plymouth. The seventeen-year-old, a man, would be later elected many times Governor of Plymouth Colony. The congregation's remarkable beginning came to be in this wise.

A young minister named John Robinson had been a Cambridge student and a brilliant scholar. Married, probably with a couple of children, he had been appointed to serve St. Andrews parish in Norwich of Norfolk. A fine preacher, he was attracting such crowds that many extra chairs had to be brought into St. Andrews' sanctuary.

But he was troubled in conscience. He could not agree with a number of recent rulings of the bishops and the magistracy. These rulings imposed certain doctrines and practices on the Church of England, to which all citizens were obliged by law to belong. Robinson slowly became convinced that the church could not really be a church at all under such circumstances. He became convinced that the church is misconceived if it is conceived as something done by reason of any outside authority.

"The Lord's people is of a willing sorte," he wrote. Therefore, they need no outside authority. The church should be entered into freely, its work supported financially by its own members, its doctrines and practices worked out by members without compulsion or coercion of any kind, under the guidance of the Spirit as the local Members should be persuaded to follow it.

In terms I used in Chapter 2, Robinson believed in religious transformation, a more or less sudden, positive and permanent change in persons, making them spiritually at home — or at one — with God, in this world and the next. He spoke of a salvific transformation in his own life and urged it in his preaching upon others. But he did not believe the validity of this experience could be at once discerned. Only the fruits of time would disclose the validity of any experience. So, he disagreed with other church reformers and radicals of the day, that a transforming — or any other — experience should serve as a test for entrance into the church. He said "the judgement of charity" is not "causelessly suspicious." The church should assume any who wished to join, "faithful, and holy in deed, as in shew pretendeth."

To understand by analogy Robinson's doctrine, recall the story of Dorothy in the Land of Oz. She was transformed in her encounter with that transcendent realm of the imagination. So were 16th and 17th century Bible-reading Puritans in their encounter with biblical myths. Robinson, however, put the emphasis, not on the transformation which happened "in Oz," but on what needed to happen after Dorothy got to be "at home" *in Kansas.* Namely: personal growth. (The phrase personal growth transposes a 16th and 17th century term: sanctification.) It was well and good, absolutely necessary in fact, for Dorothy to be transformed in Oz from a lonely and frightened child into one capable of sympathetic and courageous partnership with others. But she was, after all, when she got back to Kansas, still a child, with much to learn.

Robinson's vision of the church was of many Dorothys, of people who — having become individuals capable of courageous partnership — should now freely bind themselves into a group of promised partners in further adventures of learning and service. Again, without any compulsion or coercion, but only as they should be persuaded, through study and argument and prayer, together. He conceived the demands for growth in wisdom to require a vigorous fellowship of mutual teaching. And he held the spirit of this fellowship of mutual teaching to distinguish the true church, from all other bodies, as a unique kind of communal order sustained by the Spirit. If any doctrines were to be approved as true or any condemned as foolish, if any practices were to be commended as wise or stopped as folly, the local members would decide that, together, in their own face-to-face group.

Therefore, this church was to be constituted, not by obedience to hierarchical authority — bishop or King; not by assent to a set of propositional statements — a creed; and not by confession of a transforming experience — of salvation. This church was to be constituted by a promise, a covenant to venture, together as individuals, in the ways of the Spirit, with entire integrity.

By 1607 John Robinson had had his parish taken away, and was preaching illegally. He and others from "sundry towns and villages," searching for a better way, met anywhere and everywhere they might, now here, now there.

In 1607, meeting in the manor house of a patron in a little town called Scrooby, the congregation formed. One writer described the event this way: "There was first one stood up and made a covenant, and these two joyned together, and so a third, and these became a church, say they, etc." Bradford's account includes a paraphrase of the covenant. Wrote Bradford,

> The Lord's free people joined themselves (by a covenant of the Lord) into a church estate, in the fellowship of the gospel, to walk in all His ways made known, or to be made known unto them, according to their best endeavors, whatsoever it should cost them . . . [4]

The congregation continued for about a year to meet wherever they might. (Other radicals were doing the same;

some even met on shipboard!) Some members were fined and imprisoned. There were warrants out for others' arrest. In 1608 about 100 of them left England together for the Netherlands. They were in Amsterdam for about a year, but in 1609 removed to Leyden, probably to put some distance between themselves and other religious groups in exile from England, whose constant dissension and turmoil, over questions of doctrine and morals, threatened the whole reform movement with scandalous failure.

In Leyden they were called the Church of the Green Door. The congregation grew, numbering some 300 at its largest. In 1620 about 100 of these set sail, as Bradford said, "for those vast unpeopled Countries of America." These were the Pilgrims who landed and built their community at Plymouth, Massachusetts. Sometime after Channing's Baltimore sermon, the congregation added the word Unitarian to its name. So the congregation of the First Parish Plymouth, established there in 1620, is named to this day, now Unitarian Universalist.

The Pilgrims were, of course, much criticized for their withdrawal from the Church of England. How arrogant, said their accusers, to suppose knowledge of the true church to be reserved to themselves exclusively.

Robinson vigorously denied charges of exclusivism. He and other members did not make themselves a church because they were certain everybody else was wrong or should be abandoned as "unthinking." No, said Robinson. "Our faith is not negative; nor [that] which consists in the condemning of others, and wiping their names off of the bead-roll of churches, but in edifying ourselves."

To transpose Robinson's doctrine of the church into our terms, they were looking for personal growth in themselves which they believed could only come as they patiently practiced, together, searching out the truth, deciding on and obeying the right as it should be "made known *unto them*." They understood the fundamental note of the free church to be in the *spirit of* self-administered disciplines of face-to-face preaching, study, prayer and discussion.

A quotation from Robinson:

> If ever I saw the beauty of Sion, and the glory of the Lord filling his tabernacle, it hath been in the manifestation of the divers graces of God in the Church, in that heavenly harmony, and comely order, wherein by the grace of God we are set and walk.[5]

A question, it seems to me, of great pertinence: In such disputatious and factious times, when the charge of reactionary conservatives seemed borne out — that the congregational order was not "comely," but unstable and unworkable — when many other religious radicals *either* justified the worst conservative fears and actually wound up in destructive and violent situations *or* themselves gave up in disillusionment and reverted to submission to a hierarchical order— Why did this unlikely congregation work? And continue to work as the decades passed, in face of extraordinarily difficult decisions and trials?

Bradford, an old man, wrote his *Dialogues* on the Pilgrim Church to offer a plausible account of "the very root and rise" of the enterprise which had led them into "those remote parts of the world . . . as stepping-stones unto others for the performing of so great a work."

The "so great a work" was the exemplary establishment, for future generations, of the free church, its directions belonging to its own members. They didn't join the church as consumers of a certain amount of "fellowship and intellectual stimulation" for which they paid a token 1% of their income! Nor were they lone "I's" in "unpartaken relation" with God! Rather, they bound themselves as individuals who understood their free fidelity to each other to be the *means* of nurturing the integrity of each and of realizing the promise of the peaceable Kingdom fulfilled among them. That word "stepping-stones" bespeaks a worldview. It shows the Pilgrims understood themselves, not as seekers only, but also as participants in a historic, even cosmic struggle — for corporate freedom and excellence.

Extraordinary "stepping-stones," indeed! The marvel that they should have come to think, in opposition to the whole church/state structure of their time, that they could find the way to model free community! That they should have conceived the true church to be a thing of carefully nurtured mutuality! That they should have grasped the primary purpose of the free church to be: ever greater maturity and spiritual growth of the members! That they should have dreamed of a church constituted by a freely made promise of spiritual partnership! How unlikely, indeed!

Neither the wonder of nor the credit for these ideas belongs to the Pilgrims alone. Many another radical group had a part in the terrific historical importance of these religious concepts, eventually applied to many another social realm besides the church.

But the Pilgrims ought to be especially important to American Unitarian Universalists. They are *our* ancestors. We misapprehend our own identity, and miss out on a great richness, if we do not understand our derivation from their extraordinary spirit. I believe we could much diminish the fruitless and sterile individual-*ism* among us and instead foster together far richer varieties of authentic individuality in community, if we should, through the 17th Pilgrims, set about reclaiming, for today, a fresh, dynamic commitment to the spirit of the covenant of the free church.

A *very* brief account of how and why liberals lost this precious heritage from mind, would go something like this.

Other of our ancestors, the more technically labeled Puritans of Mass Bay, more numerous by far than the Pilgrims— The Puritans distorted the noble notion of the covenant and got off into the labyrinthian deadends of federal theology. That and an undue obsession with something the Pilgrims did not stress — namely: the exact nature of the needed transformation — led to the liberal rejection of Calvin-*ism* in the 19th century (a late label put on a calcified form of Reform doctrine which didn't yet exist in the 17th century).

Since the 19th century, in the 20th, their heirs have so consistently badmouthed the Puritans — most often with little or even *no* firsthand acquaintance with the vast literary legacy the Puritans left us — that liberals in our time are largely ignorant of our great debt to the religious radicals of the 17th century.

Calvin-*ism*, if that term is used to indicate one dead limb of the great branching work of 16th and 17th century reformers, we are well without. We need as much as ever the spirit of the covenant of the free church. What follows is intended as a kind of prose hymning of this spirit in contemporary terms.

● ● ●

Individual members of a coherent free church may be ever so singular and diverse: young or old; rich or poor; famous or little known; little schooled or many degreed; liking Bach or rock or both; pray-ers or atheist; of any race; of many backgrounds; management or labor; or changing degrees of these at different times. The more singular and diverse the better.

Individual members of a coherent free church may position themselves in any number of different patterns — of office or ceremony or ad hoc committee or study group — for different purposes at different times. Picture us in shifting, lateral designs, without hierarchy. We mean to have varying, no rigid, forms of authority.

But if the whole has integrity — and a whole *is* a thing of integrity — the free church coheres, howsoever flexibly, around a center. What is the center of the free church? And by what power are its individual members held together? What gives the free church its integrity? I offer you this answer. You will say whether it persuades.

The center of the free church, the heart of the whole thing, is a promise of fidelity, a covenant, which each member freely makes upon joining. Actually also, each member begins *again* with, or renews or re-negotiates, his or her promise many times in the course of the life of the church, in the privacy of renewed conscience or spiritual growth.

Too often our promise, or covenant, is implicit, not consciously explicit. But it doesn't really matter whether it is verbalized. It matters whether it is faithfully *meant*.

Our covenant is simply (*Simply*! What a word!) our promise that we shall *together* seek truth and support one another as we *dare*, whatever the cost, to live by the truths we cannot help believing we have found at any particular time, and to support one another in doubt in those times when we can't find or can't decide what the relevant truth is.

The free church is held together by, insofar as we live by, the spirit of this promise.

I think I should put in here that when we use the word spirit, we speak, not of anything that can be pinned down and tightly specified, nor of anything spooky either. The spirit simply (*Simply*!) is: that whole inseparable complex of ideas, understanding, memory, hope, will, learned social skills and affection — as these are actual and at once both products of and responses to reality, the results of our engagement with the world. The word spirit points to the interior life, which makes for the quality of our visible, exterior actions. The word spirit points to *that* with which we must freely cooperate to meet the conditions of our own fulfillment, or violate our own integrity.

There is a recognizable spirit of the free church. It is the spirit of persuasion. It is both free and freeing. By its fruits you know the church wherein it reigns.

I'll try to describe this spirit.

The spirit of persuasion is, by definition, has to be, can't be other than — a spirit of affection, love, for two kinds of things. It is love for other living creatures, people, and so, love for all that sustains and enriches people. And even more, it is love for truth itself, our ultimate spiritual sustenance, without which no people can long live, no matter what else they may have.

The primary characteristic of the spirit of persuasion, because it is *of* love, is this: It can only exist in a partnership of unforced mutuality with others. Therefore, it only uses methods proper to its nature, to freely given assent, to conviction, to the satisfaction of our longing for the rightness of sense and meaning and value. The power of the spirit may be — should be — vigorous and rigorous, persevering. It hangs in there! Yet though it may urge and press, it will never knowingly force. It refuses ever to be coerced itself, or to try to coerce another.

Yet, precisely because it is *of* love, the spirit of persuasion may sometimes be very angry at what — as it appears to informed and reasoning love — won't sustain, can't sustain people, angry at what diminishes rather than enriches people, angry at what is therefore wrong, sinful, deadening. The power of the spirit of persuasion can be fierce in its prophetic judgment of what *must* be changed for good to happen in people.

Yet again, precisely because it is *of* love, and because it can only exist in a partnership of mutuality, therefore, often as the spirit of persuasion is actively engaged, trying to lure, alter, move, it is just as often merely open, engaged passively, just listening, feeling, contemplating, watching and waiting, in silent stillness.

The spirit of persuasion is hardly limited, though, to either righteous indignation or quietude, though it knows both and welcomes both in their appropriate time. Rather, it moves back and forth, all the time, between the poles of needful doing and mere openness. Whatever its direction, it works *in individuals*, as each does *with* others or is merely open *to* others.

In these alternations between doing and stillness, between acting and being acted upon, consist the famous rhythms of the spirit, often compared to the movement and stillness of the winds.

Like the rhythms of the wind, the spirit of persuasion cannot *be* artificially manipulated. Attempts to divert or subvert naturally arising issues and concerns, or any effort to "work" the free life of the church according to some preconceived blueprint or set of rules, is but self-defeating. The spirit of persuasion can only be worked *in*, as a sailor at once works skillfully *with* and yields *to* the wind. It blows where it will.

And yes, we know: Sometimes the spirit of persuasion blows up a gale that destroys all before it and sometimes it is an equally killing, dead calm. We would be lying pollyannas if we did not admit this, too. Every human group, including ours, is susceptible both to false hysteria and to self-satisfied or disillusioned apathy that will go — nowhere. There are dangers and no guarantees with the spirit of persuasion.

And yet, as the winds hold out both threat and promises of rich reward to sailors, so do the rhythms of the spirit of persuasion to us.

So, in the spirit of the covenant of persuasion, in the free church each member is called to give utterance, to ask, say, explain, defend what is the truth she or he sees. To be unforthcoming is to be disloyal; for how can we learn from one another without candor! Each member is also called to yield the floor with humble courtesy, to listen, be open to, and try again and again to imagine what others see. To be unwilling or to forget to hear is to betray; for how can we receive what others may impart without their counsel! Our covenant is an abiding commitment to take and to give counsel.

In the spirit of the covenant of persuasion, as individuals together we heed our call to listen and to speak to one another faithfully *so that* — for this is our whole purpose — singly and together we may follow what we are persuaded are, better ways.

The spirit of persuasion is the spirit of a *free* religious people. It is holy to us. It holds all together, insofar as we live by it, in the embrace of the free church, in the generous embrace of people who are centered — in ever changing and responsively creative ways — around a promise of fidelity together to search for and dare to live by truth.

If the center holds, if the spirit lives, there are no limits to what we may constructively do together — for the sake of inspiration and mercy, justice, art, personal growth, or plain fun. So there are no limits to the difficulties the free church may overcome, or to the richness of its interior life, or to the effective work we may do to refashion and recreate our world.

What follows is an adaptation of the covenant of the Pilgrims, written for contemporary Unitarian Universalists, covenanted pilgrims yet, in a great religious tradition.

> We pledge to walk together
> in the ways of truth and affection,
> as best we know them now
> or may learn them in days to come
> that we and our children may be fulfilled
> and that we may speak to the world
> in words and actions
> of peace and goodwill.

Notes

1. Timothy George, *John Robinson and the English Separatist Tradition*, Mercer University Press, 1982.

2. George.

3. See George Hunston Williams, Th*e Radical Reformation*, Westminister Press, 1962; Philip F. Gura, *A Glimpse of Sion's Glory*, Wesleyan University Press, 1984.

4. George.

5. George.

Conclusion

My unabashedly passionate concern is for thriving liberal congregations.

I mean by thriving: glad, feeling gifted, just to be called to engage together in the struggle for the realization of reliable meaning; *and good at it,* good at engaging, through all the corporate arts and skills of worship, joint study and committee work.

I mean by liberal: free to practice corporately and well a wide range of arts and skills; and free to take up and pursue corporately issues — any that come up — in a very wide view of the holiness of humanity and the world.

A congregation is an organization dedicated to the realization of reliable meaning. This book of and about myths of time and history ends with an articulation of the covenant of the free church. That it does so illustrates my conviction that the organization of *any* church — liberal or any other — is a function of myths of time and history. A doctrine of the *free* church is in essence a doctrine of fidelity to the freely entered covenant. In the wide sense, it is a political doctrine, in Greek a *politeia*.[1] That is, it is a doctrine of how and why free religious people gather themselves into a congregation in the first place, and how they will work together. It, too, is a function of myths of time and history, the myths of the covenant.

Abstractly labeled, the subjects of this book have been as follows.

Chapter 1: a contemporary scholarly view of myths, a feature of historical consciousness, itself a feature of the manifest plurality of 20th century cultures; the relationship between myths and the emphases and expectations of cultures; and the role of metaphor in myths.

Chapter 2: the competing myths of contemporary religious liberals; the role of imagination in personal and social transformation; and the nature of positive personal transformation understood as the learning of some extraordinary truths, empowering covenantal partnership.

Chapter 3: the meaning of historical consciousness; the nature of corporate liberation to freedom; the conditioned nature of corporate freedom; and the nature of forgiveness.

Chapter 4: one source of contemporary ahistoricism; the structure of Western triumphalist myths; the doctrine of God, omnipotent or limited; and the relationship between costing love of justice and social direction as understood in classical American Unitarian tradition.

Chapter 5: buds of covenantal renewal in our time; Emerson's anti-institutionalism seen as traditional spiritist denial of a social epistemology; and the Reformation roots of the conception of the free church of the post-Reformation era.

My reason for taking up all these subjects is that in our time they all must be considered to deal with one subject: a liberal doctrine of the free church. Finally, my subject has been a liberal doctrine of the free church.[2]

Many of our Unitarian Universalist congregations are, at present, not sufficiently thriving, or even always liberal. The meaning of the word liberal, among religious liberals in our time, has shrunk. Among many it merely means: free to engage any issue — well, sure! Present any idea you like in our church! — but without acknowledged and careful disciplines for nurturing a community of entire mutual candor and trust, disciplines whose exercise is commonly understood as our way of practicing, together, fidelity to the liberal covenant.

Without liberal disciplines, the liberal way tends to become — not so much the specially cherished way of a faithfully free people as it is just — something you take part in if you want to, when you're in the mood, a careless style of association, liberal-*ism*. Congregations in the grip of liberal-*ism* are not free to thrive. They can't because their organization is fundamentally irrational. That is: The organization does not *follow from* a theology — or theory — of faith, a social theory of *how* we go about searching for and living by truth, together, a *politeia*.

Further, and complicating our whole situation, well-intentioned efforts to get Unitarian Universalists — an awesomely talented, caring and rich people — to shape up and work well together, especially through the structures of our Association of Congregations, the UUA— Efforts to get us to shape up and work well tend to take form in emerging organizational structures of hierarchy, which (1) imitate the management ethos of consumer oriented businesses, (2) would cause our radically liberal ancestors to bolt their graves if they could, and (3) are self-defeating because they are inconsistent with the spirit of our whole history, inconsistent with a liberal doctrine of the covenanted free church. These hierarchical structures are emerging, with little protest, because few Unitarian Universalists have ever connected two questions: What is our covenant? And so, how ought we organize our common endeavors?

I didn't dwell on our Unitarian Universalist deficiencies. They're mentioned. Long description of what's wrong — fussing — is about the most ineffective way in the world to work for constructive change. Usually, when we do "constructive criticism" — fuss — all we really do is either dishearten people or make them mad. Recounting myths — stories — which re-present the way things have come to be or ought to be is a much more effective way to work for change.

Besides, we have some marvelous congregations. We could have many more. This is a ripe time for us, a time of *kairos*, a time of singular opportunity to get our act together and soar liberally. Not "all on our own," as though we were the only liberals in the whole interdependent historical web of which we are a part. But as a distinctive people in discourse with the reformation in liberal scholarship whose central premise is the relativity of all things historical.[3]

What I have wanted to do in this book is *show* how one Unitarian Universalist takes part in this discourse and how it effects — and I do mean *e*ffects, not *a*ffects — a liberal doctrine of the church.

For reasons not difficult to understand once you dig into our history, we have never as a people achieved a broadly inclusive and rational — that is: liberal — doctrine of the free church. I started to list some of those reasons, but then I remembered you're not supposed to introduce new material in a book's conclusion.

I might summarize those reasons by citing a sentence from James Freeman Clarke, surely one of our 19th century Unitarians most liberal in every abiding positive sense. Clarke said, "We carry our churches in the power of the holy traditions which have become a part of our nature." Clarke and others whose sympathies were as broad — and there were many like him in 19th century Unitarian churches, of capacious spirit, learning, and energy — never saw the *fragility* of those "holy traditions." They could not imagine that the stories — myths — in which the corporate practice of freedom is rooted, might be lost from mind, forgot. Their defense of them was mild, not well enough grounded. And they have been forgot.

The question is: What must we do now to realize our yet great promise? Quoting the title of a reading in our hymnal from Sophia Lyon Fahs, my answer is: "It matters what we believe." And that's why, to realize our great promise, we need now to work out a broad *and broadly understood*, coherent doctrine of the meaning of liberal promises, not a creed, but a doctrine of the liberal covenant, its place in history and its summons — unto us — into the future.[4] A doctrine of the liberal covenant needs to be preached and taught, in pulpit and workshop, *in all its richness* of story — myth — and drama of personal life.

Our anthropology needs clarification, especially as it relates to the capacity to make the promise that constitutes a liberal congregation. The free church is not something "natural" people just "naturally" evolve into with age. Every child has inherent dignity and worth. No one ever loses it. We take that as given. Right. But a newborn is not neurologically able to grasp the importance of fidelity, of making and keeping promises with others. That doesn't mean we're born with something wrong with us which it takes a divine miracle to cure in *an act* of salvation. So, what kind of healthy learning — what transformation in what we hold matters, different, surely, from that we held as children — shows readiness to enter a liberal congregation?

Our ecclesiology needs clarification, especially as it relates to the meaning of Membership in a congregation or Membership in our Association. Each individual is responsible for his or her own convictions and decisions, and each congregation is responsible for the direction of its own affairs. We are never to try to coerce either an individual or a congregation. We take that as given. Right. But does that mean, if the individual owns a say in the direction of the congregation and the congregation owns a say in the direction of the Association, that participation in duly called decision-making

Meetings and financial support of duly voted programs are optional? What kind of Membership is that? Ought not the promise of Membership be a pledge of regular and ongoing participation and support? Otherwise, why join?

Our epistemology needs clarification, especially as it relates to our obligation to seek out one another's opinions, to listen to one another and to offer candid counsel, whoever has bottom-line responsibility for a decision. We say we are united in a search for truth. That is our abiding purpose. Right. But how do we learn truth, together? Is it not through comparing and contrasting and comparing and contrasting reports of experience? Is it not our fundamental, tremendous faith that we can trust truth to persuade *if* we really hear all views and sides? So, what are our organizational settings for giving and taking counsel, in ways that don't either legalistically rely on rules of procedure and job descriptions or in any manner co-opt individual or congregational decision?

Perhaps most urgently, our myths of time and history need re-formulation. We're not going to think we need to talk with others if we myopically regard ourselves as way out in front of them, on some "cutting edge." Only our sense of location *within* the universe of history can call us to participation in what's going on in our special time. Our involvement in the great religious, philosophical and political dialogues of our time needs expansion. We have been virtually isolated for too long. Our people are largely unaware of critical revision and re-interpretation of biblical and church history, which has been going on at an accelerating pace for well over a century. It's rare to meet Unitarian Universalists aware of a revolution in the philosophy of science, now two decades old. Our people don't know about the large and ever-growing literature of the Jewish/Christian dialogue, begun after WWII, or of the enormously important spread of the Christian/Marxist dialogue — or liberation theology — which may radically change South

American, African and Asian cultures. The UUA belongs to the IARF, but most of our Members haven't heard of it, much less studied to understand who are the Buddhists and Shintoists in the IARF with us.

Our women are active in feminist developments. Some of what we're doing there is wonderful. But it's not enough. We just can't claim to be a religious movement of faith in reason and expect to thrive while we unreasonably remain oblivious, as a people, to all these other developments in the religious world. We'll not be able effectively to address the world if we think we are ahead of it but are actually nearly out of it.

It seems to me we have a heavy load of work we need to do. And yet— I look for the unlikely.

I wish we had a technology that would let a writer program a book to set off an illustrative fireworks display when readers' eyes get to the real conclusion.

Loads can suddenly become light, and people — in the right spirit of faith in the covenant of persuasion — can "work mightily" and "bring forth fruit" that changes the direction of history. I'll be glad if any find this book is any help with "so great a work" as we are so extraordinarily gifted freely to take up, together.

Notes

1. For the significance of the fact that Josephus chose the Greek word p*oliteia* to describe the religion of the covenant in his *Antiquities of the Jews*, see S. Dean McBride, Jr., "Polity of the Covenant People: The Book of Deuteronomy," *Interpretation: A Journal of Bible and Theology*, Vol. XLI No. 3, July, 1987.

2. I have had — and have — no intention to write a history of the doctrine of the liberal church as it might be teased from the writings, especially of 19th century Unitarians. Any such history would have to be teased out, inferred. For no such doctrine is there e*xplicitly* present. Having once spent three months trying to identify Channing's doctrine of the church, I am ready to accept the following statement of the editors, Sydney E. Ahlstrom and Jonathan S. Carey, *An American Reformation: A Documentary History of Unitarian Christianity*, Wesleyan University Press, 1985, pp. 292 - 293.

> Ecclesiology — that branch of theology concerned with the nature and role of the Church — was never prominent in the writings of Unitarians. ...In this they were typical of American liberal theology, which maintained comparative quiet on these matters well into the twentieth century...
>
> New England Church leaders of the past had been enormously concerned with problems of polity and the ministry. The very names "Congregational, "Presbyterian," and "Episcopalian" reflect these highly divisive issues ... But in the Unitarian tradition ecclesiology was reduced to a secondary status. Men simply did not dispute about polity, the ministry, or the nature of the Church.

I have written elsewhere about the relationship between liberal *economic* theory and the 19th century liberals' assumption that the organization of the church would take care of itself. Liberal *economic* theory, in fact, was an unrecognized theology which lay behind a church polity that became more *laissez-faire* than congregational. But this is not the place to go into that argument.

3. Meanings of words change. Two that frequently change are the meanings of liberal and conservative. Operationally, in common usage "conservative" usually means: a brittle desire to conserve, not a *long* and richly flexible tradition, but the specific situation of the generation just past. Just so, as I read them, present day "conservative" Unitarian Universalists want to conserve the dated notion, of a generation just past, that we are not of the Judaic Christian tradition *and* the related proposition that the business of the church is not to criticize public policy in matters of economics or armaments.

4. A doctrine of the liberal covenant is there in the work of James Luther Adams, often honored as our great scholar and prophet, but not enough read and studied in the churches. Recent publication has at last made his work readily accessible. See *On Being Human Religiously: Selected Essays in Religion and Society,* edited by Max L. Stackhouse, Beacon Press, 1976; *The Prophethood of All Believers,* edited by George K. Beach, Beacon Press, 1986; *Voluntary Associations: Sociocultural Analyses and Theological Interpretation,* edited by J. Ronald Engel, Exploration Press, 1986. JLA is *always* concerned with the liberal doctrine of the church as a *politeia*.